Outing the Goddess Within

One Girl's Journey With 52 Guides

Anita Revel

Anita Revel :: www.iGoddess.com

Outing the Goddess Within: One Girl's Journey With 52 Guides
Anita Revel

ISBN 978-0-6151-7845-5

Concept © Anita Revel, 2006-2007.
All Rights Reserved, Anita Revel.
www.iGoddess.com

This book may not be reproduced in whole or in part by email forwarding, copying, fax, nor any other mode of communication without author permission. The intent of the author is to offer guidance of a humorous and personal nature to support your quest for emotional and spiritual enlightenment. The author will not assume responsibility for actions your undertake for yourself or others based on information in this book, especially if it involves champagne or tradesmen.

Published by Revel-ations :: www.revel-ations.com
Cover design by Flame Creations

With love and gratitude for my 52 guides:

Cerridwen, Astarte, Sri Laxmi, Hestia, Vesta, Juno, Pele, Isis, Diana, Venus, Inanna, Epona, Oya, Aphrodite, Athena, Bodicea, Brigid, Ostara, Tara, Nuit, Persephone, Hina, Amaterasu, Tyche, Circe, Freya, Hathor, Eve, Kwan Yin, Ix Chel, Rhiannon, Yemaya, Spider Woman, Bast, Gaia, Hecate, Artemis, Demeter, Oshun, Isis, Kali, Fortuna, Flora, Eostre, Uzume, Maia, Baba Yaga, Blodeuwedd, Cordelia, Ceres, Calypso, Dana and of course, my own inner goddess.

Anita Revel :: www.iGoddess.com

Table of Lessons

A quickie from the author… 7

1. Come to the edge to learn how to live 9
2. Lessons from a warrior queen 12
3. For the worthy, Sri Laxmi's gravy train 15
4. A stress puppy gets off the treadmill 18
5. Vesta and the virgins 21
6. Lusty, busty Juno gives us June 23
7. A candle-lit dinner with Pele 26
8. Isis means intuition and perception 29
9. Wild times ahead for Diana-inspired gals 31
10. Venus on the mountain top 34
11. Inanna and the gates of hell 36
12. Dream on, Epona 38
13. Aussie Aussie Aussie, Oya Oya Oya! 40
14. Aphrodite's formula for love 42
15. Athena kicks butt 45
16. Bodicea the (cricket) ball buster 48
17. Brigid says, 'light your fire' 51
18. Ostara Says, 'Wake Up!' 54
19. The measure of Tara's love 57
20. Climb aboard Nuit's stairway to Kevin 59
21. Persephone the bold… the beautiful 62
22. Goddess Hina calls for eloquence 65
23. Amaterasu's sulk of the centuries 68
24. Your good-luck goddess, Tyche 71
25. Self-reliant, like the goddess Circe 76

26.	U2? I'm a-Freya-d not!	78
27.	The mother of re-invention	81
28.	In a land before Eve	84
29.	All is love in fear and war	87
30.	The Ix Chel health plan	90
31.	Cheers to Rhiannon	92
32.	Yemaya just love this ...	95
33.	Spider Woman saves the day	97
34.	Play it again, Bast	99
35.	Get rooted on Australia Day	101
36.	The many faces of Hecate	104
37.	Living life with intention	107
38.	Gotta meet her, Demeter	110
39.	Go with Oshun's flow	113
40.	Follow that ass	116
41.	Kali vs. New Orleans	118
42.	Fortuna's Law of Attraction	121
43.	Flora's spring fling	124
44.	Happy upside-down Easter, Eostre	127
45.	The pleasure is all Uzume's	130
46.	Maia Day! Maia Day!	133
47.	Baba Yaga boo!	136
48.	Blodeuwedd the Beuwdiful	139
49.	Dial a date with Cordelia	142
50.	Survive life's cycles with Ceres	145
51.	Speaking of drunken bilge rats…	147
52.	How to have a productive affair	150

More information	154
About the author	155
Additional and cited resources	158

A quickie from the author...

The 52 stories contained herein are printed in the order in which they were published as columns – *not* in the order that the events happened in my life.

To me, this seemingly random order resonates with how we learn our life lessons. Sometimes it takes years to get the point about our experiences, while other lessons are like a slap in the guts with a wet fish – occasionally smelly, often unexpected, and usually worthy of an immediate reaction.

In any stories that are based on a co-adventure, I took the liberty of changing the names of my friends in order to protect their privacy. To my co-travellers, thank you for sharing part of your journey and your Selves with me.

I should also point out that in the spirit of illustrating a point, I have taken *some* creative license in some stories.

I did not actually swing a brown-eyed calf around my laundry to demonstrate the spaciousness of country homes, for example. That would have been cruel, and besides, my laundry wasn't really that big.

Nor did I literally eat cockroach pie – of course this is not conducive fare for the modern goddess.

So please read these stories in the light-hearted manner in which they were written. It is simply my intention to share how role models, patronesses, guides (call them what you will) can so easily manifest a basketful of lessons if you just look for them.

At the time of this book's birthing, I am still making my weekly deadline and getting a column to United Press International headquarters. Check out the latest offerings at www.religionandspirituality.com every Friday.

Love and delight,

Anita

Anita Revel

Come to the edge to learn how to live

April 28, 2006

When I left my job, I walked out with a payout of $5,000 of unused holiday pay. Not realising how long I'd be unemployed, I spent most of it on weekend jaunts, exotic chocolate and scratch-and-win tickets. The rest I squandered.

A couple of years ago, I resigned somewhat spontaneously from my job at a Margaret River winery. Life had said to me, "Come to the edge."

"I am afraid," I responded.

"Come to the edge," life had said again.

So I went to the edge, full of confidence that I would not fall. It was a leap of faith into the unknown; my future held endless possibilities. I spread my gossamer wings and leapt, stretching as far as I could, knowing full well that a chasm is not crossed in two small steps. I soared, I whooped, I felt as if I could fly forever. Oh, the thrill!

Then, I fell.

It was a slow fall. It took me nine months to hit the bottom. The crash came to pass so gradually, I barely realised it was happening. It started with a couple of unsuccessful job interviews, and then progressed to a series of applications that never even made it to interview. And it wasn't because my resume wasn't good enough — no one is more perfect than on their job application forms, after all.

It was a bit of a worry – I simply had no plans for what I wanted to do at the bottom of chasm.

At first, that was very exciting, as I decided not to limit myself by the confines of a plan. (In my experience, putting conditions on happiness only serves to prevent it from happening.) But becoming poor was not part of any plan I probably should have had. I simply had to become more purposeful about my actions if I wanted to eat more than beans on toast for the rest of my life.

So, I turned to the example set by the magical Welsh crone goddess Cerridwen (ker-ID-wen), a shape-shifting goddess of dark prophetic powers, enchantment and divination.

Cerridwen lived alone with her son on an island in a lake known as The Land Beneath the Waves. What a coincidence! I also lived alone with my son on an island known as Down Under. We were off to a good start.

According to legend, Cerridwen brewed a magical potion made from herbs and waters of prophecy under carefully monitored movements of the sun, the moon and the stars, over the course of 13 moons. Correspondingly, I developed a similar routine of intention in order to achieve my dream of finding fulfilling work.

Every morning I would read Business Review Weekly, and if I wasn't in Australia's Top 100 Rich List, I would turn to the Positions Vacant in the local newspaper. As a nod to Cerridwen and her use of the astral powers, I would also read my stars.

Invariably finding no jobs suitable for me, I began to write the Great Australian Novel. Again, considering Cerridwen, I did so under moonlight — a romantic way of saying "after my son had gone to bed and my motherly duties were completed."

Thirteen moons later, I compared my time of intentional living to that of Cerridwen's potion.

I opened my product of 13 moons' work —the Great Australian Novel — to find it was nothing more than an unauthorised autobiography. It was full of manic moments devoted to my son, his sporting commitments, cooking duties, movie chaperoning, bottle opening, bandage dispensing and all other super-mum-stuff.

Then I read it again and see that it had been a year of re-evaluating priorities, of sacrifice and discovery.

As a result of my 13-moon process, my relationship with my son has never been stronger. Now I have time to go slow and to relish the little moments of humour and cuddles. Having no income means sacrificing luxuries, but we have discovered a whole new range of economic meals, entertainment and simpler priorities.

So while it may be easy to dream about what you'd like to do, it takes a courageous person to take action and put your ideas, goals and intentions into practice. Science-fiction author Douglas Adams once spent a year dead for tax reasons, but I don't think you need to go that far. Just take that first step for the ride of your life.

Even if it does take 13 moons, "Come to the edge ... "

Lessons from a warrior queen
May 5, 2006

Jesus whipping the money-lenders? I can relate. Visualising Astarte's sword has always helped me when I'm feeling like I can't beat 'em but I'm not quite ready to join 'em.

Everyone has heard the expression "If you can't beat 'em, join 'em." But what does that mean when you're being mugged?

What if you're drowning in bank fees? Are you supposed to throw the little buoy back at the big boys? And are you supposed to *help* a bully boss sack you? No!

Well, errr, hmmm ... on the other hand, maybe that wouldn't be so bad — there is something to be said for taking your inner butterfly and laptop to the local Starbucks to fraternise with all the other 'consultants' who, like you, have chosen to "join those who couldn't be beaten."

So I'm not sure about the truth to that expression. And sure as heck, neither is the Babylonian, Assyrian and Phoenician goddess Astarte.

Honoured as the strong and wise queen of heaven, she was a warrior queen who wore the horns of a bull and rode into battle behind her horses and chariots. Forget riding a chariot into battle — have you ever tried parking one? Whoa, my horned-hat off to a gal who can do both.

With Astarte, there is no such thing as "I'm not comfortable with that" or "I'm not the most qualified person for the job" or even "I can't today, I have to thaw some karate chops for dinner." She is all about raising her sword and simply getting the job done.

In times of crisis, therefore, Astarte is an inspirational role model to look to when our creativity and self-confidence are threatened. In fact, visualising Astarte's sword has always helped me when I'm feeling like I can't beat 'em but I'm not quite ready to join 'em.

Apart from the time I used her warrior energy and landed myself on Australia's travel alert list, that is.

I was getting *really* peeved with travellers who cram every inch of the luggage carousel perimeter, you see. By crowding around that narrow, winding parade of bags, they not only block the view of the other 80 percent of travellers, but they also impede my access to my luggage as it glides past.

Seeing as my emergency corkscrew had been confiscated by airport security on a previous trip, I decided to use my bags as a weapon instead. The plan was to kneecap selfish carousel hogs on flight QF684 to Sydney.

You don't need to know the full details, but let's just say that being frog-marched into a seedy back room to face a big-bellied, droopy-mustachioed, black-eyed Mr. Honcho was not pleasant. Nor was the coffee they served. (I learned that 'instant coffee' is so named because it is only for one instant that it reminds you of coffee.)

But if we didn't have pressure, we wouldn't have diamonds. And sure enough, just in time I remembered another diamond-crusted facet to Astarte. That is, taking the warrior image too far, through hostility, only leads to self-destruction.

Explosive anger may satisfy the short-term need for revenge, but this situation in which I found myself was a lesson to exercise wisdom rather than anger. My counsel, therefore, was to examine other ways to achieve 'victory' without hurting others.

Accordingly, I marshalled my Astarte-inspired knack for making the most of a limited amount of resources. I said sorry, knocked on wood, and promptly rolled over to join those I couldn't beat — shoulder-to-jaw in the carousel gang.

Doing it in a dignified manner, with patience, respect and even a little smile, I found all these attributes came back to me threefold in the way others treated me — sans the kneecapping.

For the worthy, Sri Laxmi's gravy train

May 12, 2006

The Lord helps those who help themselves and, with only slightly different wording and altogether different emphasis, the Indian goddess of prosperity says, well... help yourself.

If money doesn't make you happy, Bo Derek says, you simply don't know where to shop.

But what if it's something other than money that would make you happy? Like being able to step into Carrie Bradshaw's (hundreds of pairs of) shoes? Then you could act like the quintessential thirty-something single gal making it in the Big City — what a dream come true to be able to swan around New York in $400 Manolo Blahniks on a $200-a-week job!

What I wouldn't give to be seen at the 'It' restaurants, acting appropriately bored at gallery openings, staying sober on six Cosmopolitans... Carrie and her *Sex and the City* protagonists could do it all.

Seeing Carrie tap-tap-tap a living on her laptop, I decided a couple of years ago that *this* was the life I wanted. Oh, to experience firsthand the energy and empowerment that New York City offered; the thrill of late nights and bright lights; the joy of wining and dining in sophisticated style; the feeling of locking myself into an apartment the size of a dog box each night.

So I packed my Prada bags, jumped on a Sydney-New York direct flight and *voila!* Twenty-four hours later, I was sashaying with purpose down Fifth Avenue. Completing the picture was a cream cheese bagel in one hand and some weird-flavoured coffee in the other. Oh the sacrifices I made!

After two hours of failing to turn heads, let alone have Mr. Big drop himself at my feet to lick my Jimmy Choos, I plonked myself down on the nearest piece of pigeon-poop to reconsider.

What was missing? I pulled my little 'Goddess Guide' out of my pocket and flicked through random pages to find which goddess was exerting her influence on me at that time. Ahhhhhhhhhh, Sri Laxmi.

Sri Laxmi, the Indian goddess of prosperity (not to be confused with wealth.) In her aspect as goddess of abundance, she helps only those who are diligent and take pride in their work. Her message, therefore, is to act with intention and passion, and to ask for what you *need*, not what you *want*.

Ha! Therein lay my clue. Can you pick it out? Go back to the fourth paragraph and read it again.

Did you see the word 'want' in there? Carrie's lifestyle is what I *wanted*, but really, it wasn't what I *needed*. Not when I had unfinished business back home in Australia.

Nevertheless, I wasn't doing *too* badly. The trip did make me realise that desires exist to guide and empower us toward achieving the lifestyle we yearn for. I had run away from the stresses of living in Sydney and tried to swap them for an even bigger city with even bigger demands. Hardly the lifestyle I *needed* at that time.

And all it took was a lack of shoe-licking to realise that the nagging voice of discontent was really a wake-up call directing me onto the right path.

I acknowledged that my path was to find a life that would be more fulfilling than the daily mondo I was currently living. Rich or poor, it didn't matter — as long as I could have health, humour and a reason to get up each day, I'd take 'abundance' as a fourth and tasty option.

With that in mind, I headed off to add a new dimension to Bo Derek's theory... I didn't find any New York stores that accepted spiritual gold coins, but I certainly found happiness in looking.

A stress puppy gets off the treadmill
May 18, 2006

In my first steps to simplifying life, I taught myself to enjoy slow Sundays. So now, instead of waking up saying, "Good Lord, it's morning!" I change it to "Good morning, Lord."

Often was the time I'd be looking forward to going back to work on Monday for the slower pace it offered. A 12-hour workday was effortless compared to the gruelling schedule of coffee, brunches, movies, coffee, golf, dinner, coffee, cocktails and putting out the garbage bins, and that was just a regular Sunday.

A typical Monday routine involved caffeinating the left brain back into action and stocking my fridge with fruit and fresh water. However, it invariably got to Friday and I would have to pour the fresh water (slightly mildewed from stagnancy) onto potted plants, and mulch the fruit (mouldy now) onto the garden — I was simply too busy to think about anything but how busy I was.

My wake-up call came when I got into work one Monday morning. I sat down at my desk as usual and started tapping Very Important Things on my computer. Without warning, I went spontaneously blind in my left eye. When I say 'blind', I mean when I closed my right eye, I was asking, "Who turned out the lights?"

The irony of my bumper sticker ("I'm a one-eyed Sydney Swans supporter") was not lost on me as I drove to visit my doctor. She was very understanding and professional as she declared me to be on a highway to hell and travelling at well over the speed limit. I simply had to slow down if I was going to live.

How does someone who is insanely busy manage to downsize stress? I once tried doing it the man's way, enduring a weekend with naught but beer, boxer shorts and the remote control, but on Monday it was too hard to kick-start the whole brain again, let alone just the left-hand side.

I did contemplate changing my habits, but if we were put on this planet to accomplish a certain number of things, in theory procrastination means I can live longer.

It wasn't until I caught a glimpse of myself in a mirror that I saw my image as 'stuck' — it was like I was frozen to the spot, immobilised by a lifestyle that resembled a quicksand pit, sans Tarzan vines at this point.

I immediately thought of the Greek goddess Hestia, the oldest daughter of Cronus and Rhea. In Greek art, she was depicted on red-figured vases wearing a veil and holding a sceptre or flower, sometimes seated, sometimes standing, but always in a pose of immobility.

Hestia speaks to women who are so focused on a situation or their working life that they are feeling inert, or 'stuck in a rut'. Their convictions keep them so absorbed in their work, they can't imagine living any other way. And here I was, in exactly this situation. Then and there I decided I wanted a Hestia-inspired existence — an uncomplicated, enriching and contented life.

By giving myself permission to retreat into my shell and explore what was really important, the introspection opened up an alternative path to travel. As Hestia maps only a sensible plan for her followers, the path she showed me seemed natural and obvious.

In my first steps of simplifying my life, I taught myself to enjoy slow Sundays. So now, instead of waking up saying, "Good Lord, it's morning!" I change it to "Good morning, Lord." I sleep in with a book and coffee-in-bed until midmorning; I stroll to the gym instead of taking my car (and *still* jump on the walking machines); and I flick on a barbecue at 4pm attracting like-minded friends who loll around with gentle camaraderie.

I have learned to see, smell, taste, listen and feel life around me, pivoting on the axis of *knowing*, giving me access to a richer life, where previously I was only an onlooker.

I now know how to run at a gentle idle instead of at 3,000 revs per minute. It takes longer to get anywhere but, hey, I have the time, and besides, the highway to heaven is a much nicer journey.

Vesta and the virgins

May 26, 2006

They're not a rock band, although they did for healthy living in Rome what The Supremes did for your soul in Motown.

I feng-shui'd my car yesterday. The steering wheel is now in the centre of the car where it will benefit most from the chi energy there. My bedroom also got a going-over. The bed is now standing in the relationship corner and I'm sleeping in the shag pile. It's the best place to find things that are hidden, like agendas, knickers and old Ken dolls. Not that the three are related in any way.

This overhaul of my important living areas came as a result of feeling cluttered and stressed. My body has a way of getting my attention when it is stressed — you know, like getting dizzy spells, sending palpitations through my chest, wearing a shower cap throughout the day...

To feel healthier, I should really pay more attention to what Roman goddess Vesta represents for modern women, seeing as she's goddess of household abundance and well-being and all.

But what if she subscribes to the Benjamin Franklin theory for health — "early to bed, early to rise" — and I have to miss out on *Sex And The City* reruns?

Ha. Patroness of wholesome-living she may be, but I do see a parallel between her Vestal Virgins and the four SATC girls, Carrie, Charlotte, Samantha and Miranda. For one thing, the Vestal Virgins tended Vesta's temple every day. Carrie et al tended to tipple every day.

Secondly, to become a Vestal Virgin was the highest standard a woman could aspire to, the role representing wholesomeness, purity and health. So, maybe it was only Charlotte who applies in this case, but if Jimmy Choos were healthy, then Carrie would win.

Thirdly, by eating right, staying active, and enjoying vices in moderation the Virgins stayed healthy and vital throughout the year. For Samantha, six dates in as many days *is* keeping the vices in moderation.

And finally, the Virgins were a powerful group of noble women who adhered to a high moral code. Hmmm, I just remembered Miranda is a lawyer — perhaps my argument isn't as strong as I first thought.

Seriously now, as Vesta's symbol is fire, I'm off to sit in front of a fireplace and ponder the stresses of the last couple of weeks. I don't really have an option — I'm hitting a wall and asking, "why me?"

Oh that, and other questions like, "why did I waste $19 to see Star Wars: Attack of the Clowns? Is it bad luck to be superstitious? Why can't I just press Ctrl-Alt-Delete and all this be over?"

There's something about a roaring fire that lets questions like these float through my consciousness and out again just as easily. The mesmerising, enlightening and warming properties of Vesta's fire lets me break free from the hurly-burly of daily life for at least a short time.

And tomorrow, if I still feel like I am only functioning from the eyebrows up, I'll feng shui the hearth and do it all over again. It's important that I do, for good health is the only cure for an early death.

Lusty, busty Juno gives us June

June 6, 2006

A little bit of love goes a long way. It moves us to risk, it spurs us to frisk; it inflames our imaginations and gives us courage to shout from the rooftops. But if it causes you to jump on a sofa on primetime TV, consult your GP.

Here comes the bride; short, fat and wide; slips on a banana peel and goes for a ride...

It's a ditty we used to sing as kids every time we saw wedding parties swanning around in the summer months — December here in Australia, and June in the northern hemisphere. But thinking about it now, it's pretty silly really. Whoever heard of a banana peel lying around in June?

The sunny month of June was named after the Roman patroness of marriage, Juno. June is subsequently seen as a fortuitous time for weddings and lifelong commitments.

Aaaahhhh, weddings. It is true to say, happy the bride whom the sun shines on, but happier the bride who can focus on elements of a relationship that are most important: loyalty, fidelity, intimacy, mutual respect, and whether the Elvis-impersonator really meant to sing off-key during the wedding service.

It's only natural that June is also a great time for thinking about other yummy stuff. Like, getting back into Aphrodite's courting phase where love means roses, diamonds, and your man not sticking his thing-oh in anyone else's thing-ee.

Yes, infidelity is a far too prevalent and sad aspect of modern relationships. And no goddess knows this better than Juno. Her husband, Jupiter, was renowned for doing the naughty in places other than the marital bed.

Juno didn't take the betrayal lying down, however (no pun intended.) This territorial wife was prepared to go to any lengths to protect her relationship and her place as Queen of the royal household — *especially* when he was off philandering.

Juno may have avenged her man's infidelities, but she was a little more grown-up about it than some scorned women might have been.

Like me, for example, when I chased my first serious boyfriend's floozy into a delicatessen. The shopkeeper was in the middle calling the cops when I stormed in...

"You want *what*?" the shopkeeper asked me.

"The SL** that has been sleeping with MY MAN!" I screamed.

What's the collective noun for floozies? A pack? A muck? A slime? Whatever it is, there was definitely a collective there — I was forced to slink away quietly when more than one woman stepped forward over the ensuing months.

Literally, Juno is the epitome of a strong woman who can say, "I deepen my willingness to give and receive unconditional love."

It took a lot of effort for me to take on such an affirmation... I would have much preferred to see a pair of scissors protruding from soon-to-be-ex-hubby's forehead. But I'm pleased to say, that 12 years later, I have embraced the protector aspect of Juno and have evolved to accept a fuller commitment to share my physical, emotional and spiritual self through union with a soul mate. Yes, I have remarried, and yes, it is wonderful.

At this high point of the year, with the energy of this patroness goddess of soul-unions at its strongest, I enjoy pondering my second marriage — the one that is going to last until death do us part.

Well, it'll be that or the credit card bill that finishes us, but at least we can say our Elvis-impersonator sang in tune.

A candle-lit dinner with Pele

June 9, 2006

I had to mobilise my inner-Pele to help me digest the fact that dinner would probably be cockroach pie.

It was while I was being stuffed down a manhole, white-knuckled with fear, that I heard the words, "don't be afraid."

No, the words hadn't come from my guardian angel. Rather, they came from a spunky urban explorer who had promised me a candle-lit evening I would never forget — exploring the inside of Sydney's storm water drains.

I know, I know. I should have known we were doomed if that was his idea of romance, but by the time I realised dinner would be cockroach pie it was too late to back out.

The activity we were embarking on was highly illegal so we only referred to each other using code-names. I figured that if courage is the ability to feel the fear and act anyway, I certainly deserved the title of Queen Courageous that night (*not* Princess Pooped-Her-Pants as some people might have you believe.) His code name? You'll find out in a minute.

Descending into the blackness of the manhole, I realised a few things.

Firstly, it is better for civilisation to be going down the drain than to be coming up it.

Secondly, they make it look so easy in the movies.

And thirdly, if the human body is the home of a woman's mental and physical attributes, the solar plexus chakra is the doorbell. When her button is pushed, it connects directly with her intuition, her fight-or-flight reflexes and her inner-Pele.

The spirit of Pele dwells inside the largest active volcano in Hawaii. She is honoured on June 11 on Kamehameha Day in Hawaii for her powers of unity, protection, creativity and change.

Change? Fairly appropriate considering I was in danger of needing to change my pants any second.

By the very nature of intuition, the transmission of thoughts through the solar plexus triggers a 'gut instinct' — the deep inner-knowledge of what is right, and what will be manifested reality. On this occasion, if my inner-Pele was right, my manifested reality would be okay as long as I didn't come across any cockroaches.

A thought created once has power, but a thought created repeatedly has greater power. I know this because once I'd started thinking about cockroaches — hello! They appeared in abundance throughout the storm water tunnels I had descended into.

And this is where my buttons got pushed. With such a fiery origin, is it any wonder Pele's energy is direct, volatile and eruptible? As was the pool of vomit I could feel sitting in my gut.

Staring into the beady eyes of hundreds of black skitteries, I had two choices.

I could either run screaming from the sewers, or I could harness the energy and direct it into a more beneficial avenue to enjoy the thrilling ride.

Imagining my inner-Pele's red-hot lava energy swirling away in my solar plexus, I asked, "does it serve my higher purpose to let my fear gush out in a spectacular explosion, or is it better to keep it bubbling away to drive me onward?"

I got to know Pele very well that night (which is more than I can say for Mr Urban Explorer.) As this goddess of fire and purpose bubbled away in the seat of my nervous energy, I made the choice to use her energy and enjoy myself.

If nothing else she certainly reminded me that, unlike the cockroaches under my feet, yes, I was alive!

Isis means intuition and perception

June 16, 2006

Is it a Freudian slip when you say one thing but mean your mother?

Mark May 28 in your diaries. For this occasion marks the first time in my life that my mother, Dorothy, told me she loves me. And here I was thinking I couldn't teach an old Dot new tricks.

One half of me is thinking, "oh, so you are human after all," while the other half is thinking, "why the HECK didn't you tell me that 37 years ago?"

My head has become a tumble-dryer for rhetorical answers, and I'm left hanging out to dry.

If I'd been brought up knowing I was loved, how would things have been different for me? What path would have revealed itself had I grown up with a healthy self-esteem and a concept of self-worth? And, is getting caught between a rock and a *soft* place any easier?

What I should have done from the start is tapped into my inner-Isis energy to listen to my intuition. That way I would have known that I was loved even if I didn't hear the words.

Isis was the Egyptian High Priestess whose esoteric attributes include intuition and perception. Her relationship with the third eye, the psychic eye, brings us a powerful skill to cultivate our trust in our own psychic wisdom. She also helps clear the clutter in your head so that you can think more clearly and see the 'big picture', which makes a nice change to only seeing laundry.

While I didn't connect with Isis energy years ago, it's not too late — I can still use her energy right now to look forward rather than dwell in the past.

To do this, I will use a pendulum. A pendulum is "an apparatus consisting of an object mounted so that it swings freely under the influence of gravity." No, I won't be using my breasts (which have an alarming tendency swing more and more the older I get.) I prefer to use a crystal on a chain for some good results.

You can use whatever tool you're comfortable with to channel the divine power. You might try crystals, cards, runes, tarot, tea leaves, psychometry, a crystal ball, firelight, water, coloured pencils on a doodle pad, or even scattered fingernail clippings (if you must) to use Isis' powerful, easy presence to understand images or impressions presented to you.

When using a pendulum, your best bet is to keep your questions limited to simple queries that require 'yes' or 'no' answers. For example, "when Jesus was a baby did he crawl on water?" would work, while "why do we wait until night to call it a day?" would not.

Firstly, ask three questions: (1) What is yes? (2) What is no? and (3) May I ask some questions at this time? The pendulum will swing in different directions to show you what is yes, no and permission to proceed.

If you can feel the presence of Isis, proceed to ask the questions you need to ask. *Trust* that the answers presenting themselves to you are correct... have faith in your inner wisdom to interpret and accept what you know deep down is true.

Wild times ahead for Diana-inspired gals

June 23, 2006

Why sit in the back seat of life when you can have all the view AND the throttle? When Diana enters your life, there's no helping it – go ahead and unleash the wild-child within.

Up until recently, I was happy with my status as pillion passenger on a friend's Harley. All I had to do was close my eyes, feel the wind on my face and pick the insects out of my teeth after the journey.

But as with all good things, they must come to an end... but only so that next time they can be better! And so it happens that I'm making the transition from motorbike passenger to rider.

I am going through this black-leather and hideous-helmet-hair phase so that next July (no, not the one that is happening next week), I can pack naught but my motorbike, tent and camera, and follow the spandex-clad wonder-bodies around *le Tour de France*.

In addition to motorbike lessons, I'm also learning Important French Words in preparation for le Tour. The word for today is *tire bouchon* — I figure 'corkscrew' is a pretty important word to know in times of crisis.

I am totally picturing myself zooming after the peloton once *le Hunky-Dories* have flashed by. I can scoot to the next town and, by the time the rest of the crew limp their way in, be enjoying latté and croissants. Or *escargot* and *fromage* — there will be no discrimination between food groups, time zones and how I match them with wine. I can see you shaking your head.

"What's got into her?" you're asking. "What's with wanting to escape onto the open road with nothing to worry about apart from the colour of your bike and whether it matches your lip gloss?"

You're really saying that? Wow.

"Well," I say to you in response, "Diana."

The Roman goddess of nature, fertility, children, harvest and wild times in the forest. *She* is what has got into me.

Diana is often depicted with her hunting dogs, deer and an archer's bow. A bit like me being armed with my credit cards, shopping list and a trusty corkscrew. Can you see the parallel?

She is also depicted in a short skirt running with her animals through the forest. A bit like me in a mini skirt running away from the animals at the Melbourne Cup. *Now* surely you can see the parallel.

The thing about Diana is that she resounds with the wild places in our inner psyche, the parts within us that hunger for more than our daily routine. The spirit of adventure-loving Diana has a way of erupting as you reach critical mass in your frustration with daily life — commando-style, if you will.

The daily-life-blues starts out with skipping book club so that you can finish a work report. Next it's foregoing a dinner with girlfriends so that you can sew a costume for Boy Wonderful. By the time you are elbow-deep in washing-up-water instead of swanning it at a post-Oscars event, Time Out seems like an impossible dream.

The good news is, Diana as goddess of the hunt enjoys pursuing her dreams as much, if not more, than she enjoys fulfilling them.

One way to connect with her energy is to take a walk in a place bursting with nature. As you walk slowly, aware of your footstep on every square of earth, pick up any stone, twig, leaf or feather that catches your eye. Repeat an affirmation such as "I have as much time as I need for myself," while carrying the gift from nature.

Either that, or take off on a motorbike in the wake of spandex-clad cyclists. Remember that Diana's energy is with you the entire day and there is no doubt you will be successful in your quest fulfil the needs of the wild-child within.

Venus on the mountain top

June 30, 2006

Perhaps the most famous and honoured goddess of the heart, this sassy goddess rules over a woman's sense of style and her appreciation for acts of love, pleasure and romance.

"It's not slutty... it's fun!" Or so says Reese Witherspoon as Jennifer Wagner in the movie, *Pleasantville*.

"Same goes for strutting your stuff and celebrating your curves," says the Roman goddess of beauty, sass, sunshine and love — Venus. Born of heaven and sea and revered for her gifts of fertility and sensuality, Venus is the embodiment of the feminine divine. Puurrrrrrrrrrrrr, kinda makes me wanna pull my fluffy leopard-print pumps out of storage and strut my stuff!

What's stopping me? Apart from a fear of heights those heels give me?

Hmmm, perhaps it's that hunching over a laptop that keeps me in my comfort zone. I like it here in my converted linen closet. It's just me and my three walls, two louver doors and the *parfum de mothball*.

The shelf that once housed stacks of unmatched bed linen is now my desk, (move over J. K. Rowling — at least you had room on your table for coffee), and the printer sits on the shelf where the pillow-slips once lived.

It's sorta like being 'in the closet' but when I finish work and shut the doors, I'm still straight. (Not that there's anything wrong with that.)

Something that was pointed out to me the other day, however, is that it is one thing to be comfortable while hunched and hiding. It's another matter entirely to exude that energy to the world, for whatever you put out there is exactly the energy you will attract.

Waaaaaaaa-haaaaaaaa! I don't want a man whose best friend is his computer! I don't want friends who prefer the company of an ASCII keyboard to real, live, enthusiastic interaction! I don't want a society that thinks its normal to adopt a *nom de plume* and role-play in chat rooms. (Although, I do have a soft spot for my Thursday 'face' of Lulu Washington — a dinky-di Aussie surf lifesaver who.... Oh, it doesn't matter.)

What I do want, however, is to be like Venus! Perhaps the most famous and honoured goddess of the heart, this sassy goddess rules over a woman's sense of style and her appreciation for acts of love, pleasure and romance. Gotta love a goddess who encourages you to do what makes you 'feel like a woman'.

Spoil yourself with a facial, spa treatment, or special outfit to wear to an art gallery, she says. Eat lunch at an elegant café; smile and laugh often; wear clothes that make you feel womanly; and adorn your ears, fingers and toes with sparkling gems. Oh yeah baby, that's what I'm talking about! Diamonds may be all the love spell I need to embody love, *become* love, attract love.

Give me Venus' energy so I can walk with a sassy step, roll my hips and stand strategically over subway air vents. It worked for Marilyn, didn't it?

Besides, I'm going with Reese on this one — it's not slutty, it's fun!

Inanna and the gates of hell
July 7, 2006

If you're a fan of the TV reality show Big Brother, *chances are you're not reading this. (I know, that's a bit like saying, "let me know if you don't get this email," but let's face it... nothing makes sense when it comes to* BB.*)*

There's a major dog's breakfast ('total mess' in Aussie-speak) happening on the Australian version of *Big Brother* this week — two chicken-livered bullies got evicted because they turkey-slapped one of the female house-mates.

'Turkey slapped'. Yes, I'm fascinated too, especially as it has nothing to do with turkeys. This is actually Generation Y jargon for whacking someone across the face with your male privates. What the...?

Now there's a bird-brained thing to write in your 'Things I Learned Today' journal. Although, if you're a decent person I'm not sure how often you'd get to road-test such a useless piece of trivia – for pig-headed folk it's bound to be a categorical shortcut to jail.

Anyhoo, the victim of this sexual attack laughed it off as hog wash. I put this down to the fact that she is still young, and hasn't yet grown into her full authentic self. Watch out for the backlash when she does. I imagine her journey will resemble that of Inanna, goddess of the dark moon and quite possibly a muse for Bob Dylan's *Knock, Knock, Knockin' On Ereshkigal's Door*.

Inanna was the Sumerian Queen of Heaven and Earth who descended to Earth to rule her people. In her quest for clarity and knowledge, she descended even further, this time to the realm of the underworld and of her sister Ereshkigal.

(Insert doom-and-gloom drum roll here.)

Turned out the road to hell was nastier'n a cow-tipper. Inanna was forced to strip off a garment at each of the seven gates until she was as nude as a bald-badger. She may have been dog-tired, but at least she wasn't turkey-slapped (that I know of.)

Each garment that was removed represented an aspect of her wealth, beauty and wisdom. Which, in *BB* Girl's case, would be like confiscating her pocket-money, pimple cream and cell phone. It was only when Inanna was near death and at her most vulnerable that she found a reserve of power she didn't know possible. Hence, she discovered new life and increased powers.

This journey involves a great deal of dogged determination and honesty with self. Only those ready to face and accept their true essence should attempt it... unless you're thrown onto this path, of course, (or fish-whipped on national TV.) In this way, when *BB* Girl is sent to hell and back by the media attention, this process will give her the unconditional power to say "no" to such intrusive and bull-dust horseplay. Naughty boys and the media alike will be told exactly where to flock-off.

Now, *BB* Girl is actually quite gutsy. So when she does get to this lowest-of-low points — and she *will* — I have full faith that it won't be too long before she's prairie-doggin' her way back to the light... perhaps right after a cat nap.

Dream on, Epona

July 14, 2006

Dreaming may well free the soul and energise the spirit, but most of all, dreaming lets you do things that would get your butt thrown in jail if you really tried them.

For the most part, many dreams are fantasy realities. Perhaps you're dreaming of an effortless promotion to CEO, for example. Or is it your dream to give a gold credit card a thorough workout at Saks, or that your 12 children are golf prodigies and can sing like the van Trapp family?

You're not going to achieve any of these dreams without a plan, some sweat, a huge amount of passion and in the case of the 12 children, a smidgeon of insanity.

It's not good enough to simply say, "one day I'm gonna..." To get where you want to go, try asking the Celtic goddess Epona to help manifest your dreams (providing they're for the greatest good of all.)

Epona is a maiden goddess who is usually portrayed as riding side-saddle on a white mare. She had a shrine in almost every stable of the Roman empire to enable safe travel and prosperous dreams.

To travel your path to fulfil *your* dreams, it helps to have a map. Start by writing a list of all the things you'd like to try before you die. I have started a list at my blog♥, but here are the first five suggestions to get you going:

- **Make a pilgrimage**. Choose a traditional destination such as Jerusalem, the Vatican or New York. Or you might prefer a site of prehistoric importance, like

Stonehenge, Machu Picchu or your primary school grounds.

- **Experience momentary rebellion**. Base jump off the top of the Statue of Liberty, sleep under the stars, or lose more money than you can afford at roulette in Vegas. As you read in my June column, I want to be an S.O.B. on a motorcycle — a big, fat, meaty beast of a bike (without a helmet to mess my hair.) That, and to get away with using S.O.B. in a spirituality forum.

- **Have fifteen minutes of fame**. Write a best-selling novel — it's a real buzz to see your name in print. Time poor? Become a news crew junky and see how often you can get your mug into their footage. Too ugly? Paint your cat's paws, have her walk over a canvas and exhibit the work as your own.

- **Believe in romance**. Send a message in a bottle. Skinny-dip in the south of France. Ride a camel into the desert. Learn how to ballroom dance properly. Memorise a poem. Shower in a waterfall. Play footsies on the Trans-Siberian Express across Asia. Pack a TV and video into a canoe and watch *On Golden Pond* while drifting on a lake — don't forget an extra long (waterproof) extension cord.

Now it's your turn to write your own list. Stop procrastinating. There are a thousand reasons to put off 'til tomorrow what can be done, well, tomorrow. But forget about them. Get Epona on your side, think of the thousand good reasons why you should just, begin.

Aussie Aussie Aussie, Oya Oya Oya!

July 21, 2006

If you're an Australian at the World Cup Soccer, don't chant the infamous "Aussie, Aussie, Aussie, Oi! Oi! Oi!" – Oya might mishear your intentions and award a penalty shot to Italy at a crucial moment.

If you could have any job in the world, what would you be?

I think African goddess Oya's job would be pretty cool. As the wife of Shango, Lord of Thunder and Fertility, they fight side-by-side creating thunder, lightning and destruction.

Don't get me wrong — it might appear as though she enjoys raining on parades, but she is actually using her powers for good. As would I if given the chance.

Oya is the goddess of storms, tempests and rain. She dances in spirals representing tornadoes and wind — the winds of change, sweeping away the old in order to prepare for the new. In other words, she wreaks destruction in order to prepare for underlying calm.

But what if you don't want a stormy road ahead? Tsunamis and hurricanes aside, there are steps you can take to avoid disaster (of the horror movie variety.)

Herewith are my top six pieces of uncommon sense.

1. Wear clean underwear — this is the key to avoid being hit by a bus.
2. Don't cook popcorn, have a pillow fight, or sleep in white underwear — you only become more visible to

the bogeyman as you run screaming through shadowy corridors.
3. If you're running away, don't look behind you, don't run down an alleyway, and don't trip and fall over. If you do fall down, get up — you'll get eaten if you lie there going "waily waily waily."
4. If you hear suspenseful cello music, get out of the water.
5. If you're alone in a house, never walk backward into a close-up – especially if you hear minor-chord music getting louder.
6. Don't fall asleep during important things. (See also: Point 1 of my 'How to Save Your Marriage' list.)
7. And finally, if you're an Australian at the World Cup Soccer, don't chant the infamous "Aussie, Aussie, Aussie, Oi! Oi! Oi!" — Oya might mishear your intentions and award a penalty shot to Italy at a crucial moment.

If you do happen to get caught up in a disaster, take heart — without rain we don't get rainbows. Yes, the destruction to your life may be a major pain in the rear, but the eventual upshot is that life will be better once you've been washed ashore.

Just remember to stay away from suspenseful music as you're sucked under, and while you're scrambling around that alleyway whining "waily waily waily," look up… you might just see a cloud with a silver lining.

Aphrodite's formula for love

July 28, 2006

Rodney Dangerfield once said that bisexuality immediately doubles your chances for a date on Saturday night. But there's a Greek goddess of love and romance that has been busting her chops since love was invented, in order to multiply your chances a zillion-fold.

I once went in search of a mathematical formula that could boil down all the elements of love and spit out an easy way to love oneself unconditionally, both in and out of relationships.

By formula, I'm not talking about a basic square root. I was looking for a deeper understanding of why we are so quick to self-judge and criticise ourselves. Perhaps a vulgar fraction might do the trick. Or a cardinal sin... uh... I mean, number. Whatever, my search revealed I'm not the only one trying to solve the most complex question of all: what is love.

A ten year University study has shown the chances of long-term love can be boiled down to two lines of algebra. James Murray from the University of Washington, Seattle, awarded points for such behaviour as humour and affectionate gestures, deducts points for negative signals such as rolling eyes and coldness, then adds it all up to predict a relationship's future with 94 percent accuracy.

Ten years? Give me a guy, a dinner, and a bill on the table and I can tell you in minutes how far our relationship is destined to go.

Albert Einstein had a much simpler modus operandi. If A = success, then the formula is X = work, Y = play and Z = keep your mouth shut. Since when did he become a comedian?

And since when did Oscar Wilde, comedian, become a mathematician? He also deconstructed relationships down to a base mathematical understanding with, "In married life three is company and two none." (Sounds like he was an accountant in a former life. Doubly so considering he also said, "Bigamy is having one wife too many. Monogamy is the same.")

It was so much easier back in the days when a skipping rope and breathless ditty could determine how many boys you were destined to kiss. That, and enough stamina to ensure you could jump your way into the hundreds.

In high school, assigning numerical values to the letters L, O, V, E and S in each partner's name was a fairly straight-forward way to come up with a number for success. The higher the number, the greater the chance of longevity. Like, until the end of next week at least.

Applying this formula to our parents, we found that 76 percent was the ideal target number — any higher or lower indicated certain divorce. A survey of my classmates showed that the 'couple most likely to succeed' was Maree McNamara and Hollywood heart-throb Matt Dillon. Despite achieving a miraculous 76 percent however, they never made it. They never even met. So much for that measure of success.

For some modern-day partner-hunters, the only numbers they're interested in are those preceded by a dollar sign. For others, it could be that a postcode is the most important number. Even the aggregate of existing descendants could make or break a future relationship. After wearing my pencil out, I finally turned to the Greek goddess Aphrodite to help me find true love.

"The answer you are looking for is *number one*," she said.

"You must always think of yourself as number one. Listen to intuition and make choices that are right for you. Reclaim your power if someone tries to manipulate you. Be your own tigress mother if you are attacked.

"Remember, your needs are important and you deserve to have them met.

"Do this by looking after number one — it is only when you have become a whole person who practices love and respect with your own feelings, that you can begin thinking about a number two."

Athena kicks butt

August 4, 2006

No matter whether you're a pouting priestess, boardroom babe, feathery fairy, earth mother or warrior woman, there comes a time when every goddess gal needs to hold up her sword and claim her right to be true to her authentic self.

When I say, Greek goddess Athena knows how to kick butt, I'm not talking about her anti-smoking habits. I'm talking about her ability to pick up her sword and defend her hometown of Athens and all that was rightfully hers.

Herewith are the seven secrets that highly effective Athena-inspired gals use to win their own life challenges.

1. Say Yeeee-haaaaaaaaaaaa... a lot. Visualising Athena's sword can be a good way to find the courage to unleash the words you have been swallowing and hence, open your throat chakra. Screaming "yeeee-haaaaaaaaaaa!" (Dukes of Hazzard style), helps lubricate your voice so that words can flow easier. It also helps get your car across impossible crevices and over unruly crates.

2. Blessed are the peace-keepers... sometimes. Athena's lesson is to release your habit of biting your tongue in order to 'keep the peace' — do you think she could have saved Athens had she given way to her attackers? I think her words would have been more along the lines of "χαθείτε σας δυσάρεστοι Ρωμαίοι" – without the 'f' word though.

3. Feel the Love... for yourself. If you're coming from a place of cast-iron self-love and self-worth, no-one can

topple your balance. In a poll at Goddess.com.au, 78% of women believe the most beautiful woman in the world is not Paris Hilton, Lucy Liu or Janet Jackson — the most beautiful woman is actually in the mirror. Coming in at second place is Sophia Loren... what a great role model for style, grace and unbeatable Athena-esque resolve. She is in good company coming second to the Goddess Gals ;-)

4. Disarm criticism... with a smile. Criticism, schmiticism. Athena had the head of Medusa on her shield to turn her critics to stone, but the same immobilising effect can be achieved with a disarming smile. You can defuse tense situations (such as a Trojan War) with a disarming smile (much easier than building a wooden horse.) Smiles are infectious, so the more you smile the more you will be infected by positive vibes and the subsequent 'can do' mindset.

5. Toot your own horn... loudly. My mother always said, "to do something properly, do it yourself." I think that's why I've learned to live with a pile of dirty laundry and a housecleaner. But I do have other traits I don't mind spruiking, Athena-style. To get started on your own list of star qualities, start by writing down all the positive adjectives you can think of that start with the first letter of your name. Then turn these words into affirmations: e.g., Anita is adventurous, adorable and absolutely ummm.... *ravishing* (not to mention creative!)

6. Rally your troops... and side-kicks. Athena appears in Greek mythology as a helper of many heroes including Hercules, Jason of the Argonauts and Odysseus. She

didn't accrue these allies without being tough herself. So if you want to be surrounded by the kick-butt energy of Charlie's Angels-style pals, pull on your thigh-highs and step out loud and proud. Some good "yeeee-haaaaaaas!" will help you leap into action (and hotted up convertibles) so you can find like-minded allies to help you achieve your goals.

7. Declare war... against clutter. There is as much satisfaction to be found in simplicity as there is in resolving complexity. If you have clothes in your wardrobe you haven't worn in a year, give them away. If you have books on your shelf that you know you are not going to read again, pass them on. What junk is lurking in your drawers that you haven't used (or even laid eyes on?) Just as Athena threw out her enemies, throw your junk away!

Anaïs Nin once said that life shrinks or expands in proportion to one's courage. To grow into a life bursting with possibilities, connect with your inner-Athena.

Oh, and say "yeeeee-haaaaaa!"... a lot.

Anita Revel :: www.iGoddess.com

Bodicea the (cricket) ball buster

August 18, 2006

Bookmakers, drug tests coming up dirty, marital infidelities, terrorism – it's time to put Bodicea into the game to clean up Australian cricket.

We have a cricketing legend here in Australia by the name of Dean Jones. I've had a crush on him for as long as I've had leg hair — he's good-looking, gentlemanly, and can somehow ripple his muscles over a bat in a most alluring way.

But he got sacked by the Dubai-based Channel Ten Sports recently for referring to the South African Muslim cricketer, Hashim Amla, as a "terrorist." Fair enough, some might say. No-one deserves to be slagged off for their race, religion or preference for hand-bags.

But compare his story with that of another cricketing ball man, Shane Warne — the Don Giovanni of the sporting world. Check the contents list on the 'Shane Warne' page at Wikipedia and this is what you get.

1 Career

2 Controversies
    * 2.1 Bookmakers
    * 2.2 Positive drugs test

3 Personal life
    * 3.1 Marital infidelities
    * 3.2 Endorsements and Off-field fees
    * 3.3 Cars

4 Recognition

5 Sledging incidents

Bookmakers, positive drug tests, marital infidelities, sledging... what kind of moral character have the cricketing big shots got if Dean Jones gets shafted, but Shane Warne gets to carry on?

Bring on Bodicea, I say — the great Celtic queen who amassed an army of 20,000 Celts to execute revenge for the rape of her two young daughters.

If Bodicea could cut a path of ruthless destruction through the province of Brittania and kill an estimated 70,000 soldiers of the Roman Governor, then imagine the revenge she could take on behalf of the 1000 women Shane ('Horny Warny') Warne claims to have slept with... broken fingers on his bowling hand; a nasty disease on his middle wicket; death by drowning in a pottage of his beloved baked beans.

At this juncture, it is worth noting that the only difference between Shane Warne and Don Giovanni is four. Giovanni, the libertine in Mozart's opera of that name, kept a log of the ladies he had bedded (1003 in all.) The fagging, shagging Warny only needs to bed another four women and he will have a new record on his hands. Stay tuned — no doubt you will hear about it by text message soon enough.

Back to Bodicea. Her energy manifests in women who want to scream, maim and kill with superhuman energy. Like me, every time I see this Mega Gig's mug on the telly or his verandah-hanging-over-grotty-underpants in yet another newspaper.

But what to remember with Bodicea is, in this day and age, killing someone is not only highly illegal, it also makes a terrible mess on your carpet.

So the thing to do is, channel her energy in a way that is going to achieve something positive. Like teaching your sons that this sticky-wicketed sleaze bag is an anti-role model. Or starting a petition to have Dean Jones reinstated. Or boycotting cricket matches until each and every one of the thousand women he maligned receives a personal apology...

Actually, I take that back. Just boycott cricket matches unconditionally! There are far better ways to waste five days of your life... like, writing a column about the scourge of sport, for example....

Brigid says, 'light your fire'

August 25, 2006

Up until yesterday, I felt as though my future was like a lava lamp – fun to look at, but not very bright.

Up until yesterday, I felt as though my future was like a lava lamp — fun to look at, but not very bright. I was missing my normal pep — my zing, my sparkle, my Bruce Springsteen CDs.

I was like a man reading a map... directionless. It happens. The ebb and flow of energy has to happen for there to be balance in life. With the good comes the bad; with the night comes the stars; with the champagne comes the... hmmm, can't think of *anything* bad about champagne.

It was something I was thinking about while strolling along the beach one evening last week... my lack of goals, that is, not the champagne (although that came a close second.)

What I needed was a new direction in life. So I turned around and headed north instead of south. It was only a small thing to do, but it was something to change my outlook. It wasn't going to give me a reason to leap out of bed in the mornings, but at least I'd taken the first step in challenging the rut I'd found myself in.

Then, feeling rather smug and altogether too pleased with myself, I took my rut-challenge one step further... I decided to confront a fear.

While standing on that beach looking into the setting sun doing its melted-butter-plop thing into the Indian

Ocean, I chose to confront my fear of cold water. It must have been the change of direction that made me want to step out of my safety zones and into that surf, ah, I mean, frozen ice particles. I was still defrosting 24 hours later.

But it was the best thing I ever did for myself because while I was ankle deep in my battle over this fear, I looked up and was speechless at what I saw.

Less than 15 metres off the shoreline was a collective noun of dolphins in a frenzy of catching their dinner. There must have been about 12 of them, or maybe 20, or 50, (but as this story is still young I'll say 12 in order to give it room to grow later on), gracefully lolling about in the water one second, recklessly diving the next, and dancing on their tails as dinner disappeared down their bottle-nose gullets the next.

I forgot all about the numbness in my feet, and stood mesmerised by this spectacular show. As though magnetised (like ET being called to the mother ship), I walked out deeper into the water until I was amongst their majestic graceful forms darting all around me.

It was a truly magnificent way to spend 20 minutes — it even took my mind off the puzzling question: how deep would the sea be if they took out all the sea sponges?

By this stage, the sunset was a flaming pallet of reds, crimsons and purples — an enormous fire raging on the horizon. Fire being a symbol of the Celtic goddess Brigid, the penny dropped. As patroness of light, inspiration and all skills associated with fire, she had brought me to this place to gift me with her healing powers.

I allowed myself to explore the flames over my head as I asked her for guidance out of this maze I had created for myself. That, and where I could find my lost CDs.

Sure enough, it came... the spark I had been looking for to fire up my passion for life again. Just a flicker at first, a faint hope, but it grew and grew until it was a blaze big enough to dry socks in front of.

And just look at me now... In the words of Bruce Springsteen, "Oh, oh, oh, I'm on fire."

Ostara Says, 'Wake Up!'

September 1, 2006

Here in Australia on the first day of September, all creatures are testing new fur, feathers, scales, teeth, claws, skateboards and tennis racquets and heading toward the revitalising light of Spring.

It is the first day of Spring here in Australia. Primal urges to reproduce are kicking in, as are prevailing urges to clean the nest.

Talk about reproductive urges — hooly-dooly... on one hand, my Golden Retriever became a daddy this week to eight adorable hungry pups. On the other, my 12-year-old Boy Wonderful asked me why I don't have any condoms in my bedside table.

Tragic isn't it? Being bailed up by a 12-year-old about responsible birth control. Kids are just growing up too quick these days — he informed me yesterday he was already considering which retirement home to put me into...

Like I said, primal reproductive urges and cleaning the nest. There's no helping either of these compulsions when Spring arrives.

For us goddess gals it's a time to stretch, yawn, awaken and chuck off the winter blues. At this time, we reach upward, outward, flex and gravitate to the light (providing we can come out from under the doona.)

When I say, we gravitate to the light, well, I don't mean the 'dawn' type of light... not just yet anyway. Tell me, if getting up at sunrise is so natural, why were alarm clocks invented?

Instead, I've got a goal to become a dawn riser by about our Spring Equinox on 23 September. To help me connect with my inner-early-riser, I'm calling on Ostara's energy.

Ostara is the maiden goddess in German mythology who is celebrated when night and day are equal and balanced, (unlike my brain at any stage before coffee.)

Her name means 'movement toward the rising sun'. Mine must mean 'movement towards the underside of the doona' and hence I have trouble getting up in the mornings.

Here are some tactics I'll be using to get me up and at 'em each morning which you're also welcome to try. Think of it as 'dawn boot camp'. Or if you're of a more fragile nature, 'the sunrise fluffy-slipper retreat'.

- Wake up at the same time... no, not at noon as per my winter custom. Set a time midway between where you *aspire* to get up, and the time where you actually *can* get up. Gradually put the 'snooze' button further and further out of reach until you're either falling out of bed on one side or you're sprawled all over Mr. Right-For-Now on the other. With any luck it'll be a case of 'wakey-wakey-hands-off-snakey' for all concerned.

- Think 'Benjamin Franklin'. Mr Franklin is considered the Father of Daylight Savings, and not just because he succumbed to primal reproductive urges. No sirree, he noticed that if he went to bed earlier that not only would he save on candles, but he could add extra daylight to his life by waking earlier. Genius huh? All it means is, blow out your candle at dusk and errrr, well, what you do after that is your business I suppose — just be ready to do it all again at dawn. ;-)

- Touch your toes... Prying open the eyes is exercise enough for me in the first stages of 'dawn boot camp', but generally, real exercise is a great way to wake up. Aim to build up a fitness regime in the mornings to get the blood pumping — try touching your toes, a couple of star jumps and stirring your coffee extra vigorously.
- Dream on... Even if you're still engrossed in that dream where Brad Pitt and Orlando Bloom are demonstrating wanton reproductive urges, get out of bed and sleep-walk to another place where you can continue to indulge in such a delicious dream. If you can hang onto this dream, whatever you do not, *do not wake up!*
- Sleep like a baby... wake up every three hours with a pooey nappy? Hmmm, perhaps we'd better scrap this last tactic.

Hey, tactics for getting up at dawn? What am I worried about? I've got the best inbuilt motivator right here on my doorstep — with eight Goldie pups to look after, I'll be up at dawn every morning no matter what! Thanks Ostara!

The measure of Tara's love
September 8, 2006

Ever since Spring arrived in Australia, I've been positively BURSTING with new energy. Which sure as heck beats negatively bursting with it.

Spring is here. New-born lambs are skipping around their paddocks, close friends are announcing pregnancies, and my hairdresser's phone is constantly engaged. It's time to think love, love, lurrrrrve, and for that, I think of the Tibetan goddess, Tara.

Spanning Hindu and Buddhist traditions, Tara is a goddess of compassion, love and eternal energy (*sans* batteries.) She reminds us that all things pass, and, unlike my winter-blown hairdo, each moment is perfect.

It is said she can be invoked under her 108 names on a rosary of 108 beads. It's as if 108 represents the measure of her love... Interesting. If you were to think about Tara in terms of numbers, this is how I calculate Tara's effect on my life.

- When I am prepared to go to the 'enth degree in my love life, then my number is 180. That's how many degrees my attitude to relationships has turned around since inviting Tara into my heart.
- If time flies when you're having fun, then add another 1,642. That's how many days of loneliness that have been forgotten since I've known Tara.
- If love sets your heart racing, then I deserve a ticket for exceeding the speed limit. For rushing headlong into new and meaningful connections, 120 is the dollars I

would be fined; three, the number of points I would lose from my license.

- If love were fluid, add another 500 to the measure. That's how many litres of jelly would fill a wrestling ring. Love is, after all, like jelly – fun to roll around in, but the more you try to hold onto it, the more it squeezes out of your grasp.
- If love is blind, my number is twenty. Having learned from experience, my eyes are open, my vision twenty-twenty. I am prepared to see and accept what is real, not just what I want.
- If I give love, I get more in return. So at the current market rate, add seven percent compounding interest to any investment I make in helping love grow.
- If love is built on solid foundations, I have just turned my first clod. But I know my castle will reach to the stars, a shining monument made up of the 1,000,000 bricks of love gifted by Tara.
- If love could be measured by tensile strength, then less is more. No matter how strong you are, you can't hang on to something that doesn't choose to stay. The only way to hold on to love is with open arms.
- If the lengths one is prepared to go to in order to nurture love, are a measure of love, then Tara's love is immeasurable. That's how many lives she has touched with her compassionate love.
- If love gives you wings, then I have no number. There is no measure of the dizzy heights love can carry us, the thrilling rush of attaining new degrees of openness. Open your eyes to the *now*, says Tara, and while you're at it, have yourself a Self-Love Affair[1].

Climb aboard Nuit's stairway to Kevin

September 15, 2006

I was as sad as the next person with the passing of the Crocodile Hunter, Steve Irwin, last week. But I did achieve some comfort in realising that, crikey, they're sure having some fun in heaven now that he's there!

Brooding over Crocodile Hunter Steve Irwin's death last week, I headed outside last night to clear my head and look at the stars. As the Egyptian goddess Nuit is typically depicted wearing a cloak of stars that act as a gateway between heaven and earth, to me the stars represent her divine connection between earth and cosmic light.

As I followed the blazing trail of the Milky Way, the stars seemed brighter than any time I could remember. The clusters and random sprinklings of celestial bodies reminded me of something... a vision of some sort... No, not a vision of the Virgin Mary — of late she has only revealed herself in a grilled cheese sandwich, through copious olive oil tears and in a pile of random chocolate drippings. (What is it about food and women? Must have something to do with out-of-the-ordinary pregnancies.)

It must run in the family. Mary's son has also been busy revealing himself as a Baby Jesus Cheeto in a Jesus Frying Pan, and even via a John Paul II chicken breast. (What is it about *men* and food? It's not like it's their religion, is it?)

And as for the latest divine revelation... at least it wasn't a 'Not Fake Jesus-On-The-Cross Stone' — a Jesus-encrusted beach pebble which appeared on eBay this morning. I love that it had to be pre-empted with "Not

Fake" — I might have been scrambling for my credit card otherwise.

The seller from San Jose, says "...I collect shells, stones, fossils and other things in nature. So when I found this Jesus stone I showed to a lot of people and they too saw the Lord right away. It is Jesus on the cross, look and you will see his arms out to his sides and what looks like blood on his chest, and the thorns are seen upon his head."

The seller figures that if someone would pay $28,000 for a piece of Mary-toast, then you would similarly fork out for this stone. All you have to do is "...Look at this photo good, Look deep into the stone..." to see the Lord's image. It is worth more than gold, apparently, but perhaps mainly because, "I need the money," according to the seller.

But enough of eBay and the virtual warehouse of endless items of faith. Unless, of course you want to talk about shoes, then I'm on my knees and praying for all soles.

Let's get back to the cascade of stars streaming across last night's sky.

As I said, I was mulling over the meaning of Steve Irwin's death, and feeling immensely saddened for his family, whom he adored. It was at this point I saw a vision and began to ramble.

So... suddenly I was able to make out the vision. The stars were forming a stairway to Kevin — another larger-than-life excitable Aussie who's already up there — Gold Coast businessman 'Big Kev' McQuay who was famous for his catch cry, "I'm excited."

It was then I broke through the weight of my grief with a giggle.

Yes, a giggle. You see, Nuit's esoteric attributes are those of oneness, bliss and universal love. She helps us bond with our planetary family while her cosmic energy acts as our bridge to the realm of cosmic consciousness. Therefore, when drawing on Nuit's energy, many people experience a contact with a guide, whether by voice, automatic writing, or other stimulus.

For me on this particular occasion, it meant that I was able to receive a message from beyond. It was as clear as a bell and funnier'n my dog eating black-cat lollies.

The message was... "Crikey, I'm excited!"

I just hope this doesn't mean heaven is a warehouse full of crocodiles... Not even on grilled toast.

Persephone the bold... the beautiful

September 22, 2006

What does it take to be queen of your own drama? And is it possible to be a drama-less Queen? We'll find out, after this break...

Following my own advice, I keep a journal on my bedside table. If I ever wake up with a vivid dream or a brainwave I record it in the journal while it is fresh. If I ever wake up with a hunky mate, on the other hand, then I... uh... never mind.

Anyhoo, I once dreamt about a love story of epic proportions. There was a man, a lady (not that there's anything wrong with that), and lots of love hearts, intrigue, passion, comedy, intensity and shoe stores. I'm telling you it was the love story of the century, only without a gin joint.

I snapped awake from this dream bursting with openness, joy, and the overwhelming need to go to the toilet. I also wanted to sing about music being alive with hills, but it didn't make sense.

Once back from the loo, I quickly jotted down the story and went back to bed — I was happy that sleep would be easy now that this story was safely preserved in my journal.

The next morning I could barely wait to read my love story... Here is what it said:

Jack meets Jill. They fall down hills and climb in love.

Alright, so that exercise didn't work. Not in this instance, anyway. But I'll tell you about another time that it did work out for me...

This story I wrote was about Persephone (purr-SEF-own-ee) — the maiden goddess who was kidnapped to the underground by Hades. It goes like this:

"I don't want to go with you," said the young maiden.

"The choice is not yours to make," the Dark Lord replied. "It is your destiny."

(Deleted Scene: The young maiden hugged her cloak around her shoulders, covering her budding breasts and pearl white décolletage. It made no difference — despite the warmth remaining in the late summer day, she still shivered.)

A single tendril of auburn hair fell across her angelic face as she looked away from his powerful, evil eyes. Long lashes fluttered, blinking back the grief at the prospect of leaving behind her green and vibrant world — true to the prophecy at the time of her birth, he had come to claim her as his bride.

She contemplated the trail through the woodlands which lay ahead of her. Strange, she had never seen it before. She knew it led to the Underworld, the realm of the Dark Lord, and that it was time to go and live in his macabre world of darkness. If she denied him, his wrath would wreak havoc, famine and destruction on the world.

With one quick glance behind her, she bade farewell to the forest folk. Then, with her regal chin held high, she headed down the path to manifest her destiny.

Phew... exhausting huh? Naturally, I was pretty horrified when I woke up to read this the next morning. I mean, if there was ever an award for cheesy drama, I'd written the gold trophy. But I *did* learn something from the exercise.

According to the real mythology of Persephone, she was indeed abducted by Hades whereupon she took on a dark and mysterious persona as his wife and Queen of the Underworld. Although her grieving mother, Demeter, eventually found her, Persephone had eaten some pomegranate seeds effectively binding her to the Underworld. Thereafter it was agreed that she would divide her time equally with her mother in the spring and summer, and her husband in the autumn and winter.

Or, as we understand the seasons in modern times, she came up for the season of outdoor concerts and ballgames, and went back down for the season of nothing-on-TV.

As the Equinox flits past this weekend, Persephone is now emerging from the Underworld here in the Southern Hemisphere, and descending back into it for our Northern cousins. You see how her energy is in constant motion from light to dark, dark to light?

Light to dark, dark to light. Sounds like me on any given day, really. But consider this energy and how it works in you. The key to making the most of this perpetual energy in motion, is to be unafraid of the dark energy when you inevitably come across it.

Call it listlessness, depression or shoelessness, but Persephone's message is to make friends with your shadow self — that side of your persona that is normally hidden from the light of day. In achieving balance and acceptance of all aspects of your personality, you get to experience what it is to be a drama-less Queen.

Goddess Hina calls for eloquence

September 29, 2006

The Australian government spends zillions preaching the dangers drunk driving. I would like to see a new push espousing the dangers of dialling while under the influence. The campaign would be called: "If you drink and dial, you're a mobile idiot."

Here in Australia, we are a nation of happy little SMSers, but it's mostly females who are the culprits. And we get worse the more we drink.

Or is it that we get better? If you've been hiding in your cocoon for a while, champagne has a way of turning us into beautiful butterflies, both in our own minds and in those of the beer holders.

Furthermore, we begin to *feel* like butterflies... Thumbs become a blur as they float and flit over the phone keys, and we become gifted with titty wête-à-tête.

Often's the time I am transformed into the butterfly goddess Hina — the Pacific Islanders' messenger, carrier of news and creator of ideas. Whipping her followers into vigorous idealism, Hina's speeches vibrate with inspirational energy. A bit like my SMS messages really, only without the whip.

Wordplay becomes foreplay as I bombard the objects of my affections with cheeky SMS messages. Once, I even sent a series of flirty messages to a random number in a modern-day version of the message-in-a-bottle.

It was all good — I think. It's just that I couldn't read the reply. What normal person understands "QT ~:o 1chu" really means "Cutie baby, want you?"

Be it a message sent once, or 48 times in a five-hour period, it seems funny while champagne is bamboozling your sense of humour. I even used to brag about it to my friends — "And then I texted him when I was drunk! Ha ha ha ahah haa."

As a communicator, Hina's inspiring speeches and ideas give birth to new ways of thinking. Must be her influence then that SMS requires mastering the art of text-speak... If you're a beginner, you can always use this tool* to transl8it!

iz simpl 2 uz! jst typ n yor SMS, TXT o ch@ spEk & Lt transL8it! cvert it 2 pln eng —o— typ n a frAze n eng & cvert it 2 SMS TXT lingo! bcum a mmbr 4 frE & U 2 cn submit yor defintnz & phrAZs

If that's not bad enough, then there's the issue of driving your address book.

Sending a message like "Luv ya long time G.I. Me so need u!" to Dave is fraught with danger if Dave is only one step away from Dad in your address book.

So what is the solution? I suggested to a friend, a particularly bad offender for drink-dialling, that she hand her phone to her responsible host upon arrival at a party. The host would hide the phone until such time Sandra could prove her sobriety, no matter how many hours (or days) it took. This solution worked fine.

---

* www.transl8it.com/cgi-win/index.pl?convertPL

Until the host got drunk and used Sandra's phone instead of her own and sent drunken SMSs to the whole world.

Sandra has since been added to the subscriber list for 'SMS Anonymous', 'Sex Addicts Support Group' and 'Big Bad Toy Boys', with no clue of how to unsubscribe.

For drink-drivers, the fallout of their transgressions could be a fine, or jail, or a lifetime of soul-crushing guilt.

But for drink-diallers, we're looking at ostracism from friends, guilt for triggering marriage break-ups, or a lifetime of daily messages from big bad toy boys looking for some fun.

Hey, wait a minute. That can't be all bad, can it?

Amaterasu's sulk of the centuries

October 6, 2006

You want to rant and rave, Peacock? One Japanese goddess says it's completely okay to do so.

How come we can never just *rant* or just *rave*? Why do we always have to do both?

I certainly did both when I found my boyfriend-du-jour cheating on me. I waved him out of my life with my thumbs in my ears, fingers wiggling, tongue wagging and eyes crossing. Good to see I kept my dignity.

After he'd gone, I hammered my fists onto the nearest wall, gritted my teeth and released my pain through sound — a primal scream that was enough to wake the dead. In fact, it was such a volatile mix of emotions — the anger, the remorse, the denial — I almost wanted to join the said dead.

But most of all, I felt absolute weariness at the thought of spending yet another seven years hating men. It was not something I wanted to go through again, and definitely not for the sake of someone who's not at least an ex-husband.

Three days later I was in the waiting room of my counsellor, flicking through last decade's magazines. She called my name while I was in the middle of an article describing how Mad King George III went through a stage of ending each sentence with 'peacock'.

It was fascinating, giving me a warped sense of hope: There has existed someone worse off than me.

"Oh, that's interesting," the doctor nodded upon hearing my story. "It sounds like something that will either kill you or send you crazy. I should know. I've been through it myself."

Lowering her notepad and picking up her prescription pad, she continued.

"What you need girl, is a dose of giggles. Get out of your cave and do something that makes you laugh so hard you want to pee your pants."

I realised that what she was saying was absolutely right. Not the bit about peeing my pants, but the bit about if we can laugh at our situations we can survive the terrible things that happen to us.

Her analogy of the cave got me thinking about the Japanese sun goddess Amaterasu.

In what has to be the sulk of the centuries, she hid in a cave to get away from cruel realities in the world. She stayed there, depressed and grieving and refusing to come out. Without her there was no sun, the rice fields lay dying in the endless night and the people grew hungry.

Fortunately, the goddess of mirth, Uzume, knew that a sense of humour is one of our most powerful stress coping behaviours. It brings in oxygen, vibrates the internal organs thereby increasing oxygen absorption, causes muscles to contract and increases the secretion of peacocks. Uh, I mean, endorphins.

Uzume rolled a copper mirror to the front of the cave and danced wildly on an overturned tub. Hearing the commotion and overcome with curiosity, Amaterasu came out of her cave. She saw her radiance reflected in the copper mirror and began to laugh at Uzume's antics. Her grief dissipated, her brilliance returned to the world and life was renewed.

What I learned from Amaterasu's story is that laughter empowers us in hopeless situations and gives us a sense of control when things around us seem crazy.

Just like Amaterasu, people who look for the bright side gain physical, psychological, and spiritual benefits. If nothing else, the view outside the cave is certainly brighter.

Peacock.

Your good-luck goddess, Tyche
October 13, 2006

If you're dreaming of luck this Friday the 13th, wake up -- the sooner you start work, the sooner you'll get lucky.

Are you the lucky bird that got the worm, or the unlucky worm that got 'got'? And what does that mean for "good things come to those who wait"? It may be good news for the worm, but the early bird goes hungry.

Good luck is all about perspective, says Richard Wiseman, a psychologist who says looking on the bright side makes you luckier in life. So if you're a bird, go for the former proverb, and if you're a worm, the latter.

Richard has come up with four principles of luck.

1. Expect good luck
2. Create, notice and act on opportunities
3. Listen to gut feelings and act on hunches
4. Turn bad luck around by imagining how it could have been worse.

How it could have been worse? What's this bloke on about?

What's worse than having every size-7 crystal-studded slingback in the store missing its pair or sold out? What's worse than reaching the strawberry at the bottom of a champagne glass to find half a worm? What's worse than your son telling you the cat likes to drink water from the toilet because it's tasty — I mean, how would he know it's tasty?

I once read in a feng shui book that it is bad luck to sit under a skylight. I figure that's just common sense — you don't want to be sitting there if Spider-Man were to come crashing through. Or would that be good luck? After all, the commotion would earn you a morning off work, a week of gossip by the water cooler, and who knows — Spider-Man might turn out to be the man of your dreams (providing he didn't get squished in the fall.)

No matter what your belief about luck, having good luck is basically *believing* that you're lucky. It's also about working for it – Thomas Jefferson says, "I'm a great believer in luck, and I find the harder I work, the more I have of it."

And, being lucky is about being nice to Tyche (pronounced tee-chee), the Greek goddess of fortune.

A bit of an idle idol, it is said she would run about juggling a ball rather than carry the cornucopia filled with golden fruit. When she did turn her attention to the fortunes of mortals, Tyche bestowed protection, success, prosperity and good luck on those who asked for it.

Or not, depending on her mood. Which would explain why the French say, "A person is unlucky who falls on his back and breaks his nose." I suspect she was feeling capricious the day that proverb was crafted.

As further testimony to her fickle manner and the volatility of life and luck, the first set of dice were found in Tyche's temple. As were pink feathers, sequins, some Monopoly money, and a solitary size-7 crystal-studded slingback.

Just my luck.

A looove song for Goddess Ishtar

October 20, 2006

Learn to love your tea-pot. Ah, I mean, curves.

The worst thing about getting older is that while my mind is finally getting itself together, my body is falling apart.

Not that I'm fat — I'm more of a nutritional over-achiever. It's just that, well, I'm feeling kind of flubbergasted — as in, aghast at the extra flubber. I have put on 18 pounds in the last 18 months. Weight gained, mind you, *in spite of* the girth control strategies I have in place.

I accept that I love food too much to starve myself. Besides, one eating disorder in a lifetime is one too many, (even if it did happen every Good Friday when going hungry was preferable to eating Mum's salmon patties.)

There's always ex... ex... exercise. (ughghghhghgh, why isn't that word four letters long?) When I think of exercise I think of regimented rows of lycra-clad soldiers all hailing their aerobics instructor. Step two three four, and back two three four! Talk about exercise Nazis...

Time has come to implement a plan. If I can't starve and I won't exercise, there's only one thing left to do: learn to love myself just the way I am.

Now, life may be short, as they say, but I happen to believe it is the longest thing we have. And in our lifetime, the person with whom we have the most enduring, honest, longest-lasting relationship is our Self.

Mohammed Ali got it right when he said he said, "I'm not the greatest; I'm the double greatest." Now there's food for thighs. I feel it is particularly apt seeing as I feel double what I was — particularly around said thighs.

But enough of the self-effacing talk. According to the Babylonian goddess Ishtar, being 'double great' would make me double sassy, doubly inspired and infinitely lovable.

Ishtar is descended from the goddess of romance, Venus, and her energy encompasses all that is 'woman': nurturing mother, inspired companion, playful bed partner, wise advisor, insightful leader, dear friend, wild woman. To this list I add, easily confused in the supermarket.

To energise myself with her divinely feminine energy this week, I dressed myself in clothes and jewellery studded with her symbols such as stars, the moon, the lion or the dove. I took my drum outside under a full moon and I began to play.

I felt my heartbeat reverberate through my shoulders, arms and hands to the drum. I delighted in the infinite power of connection to the earth as the vibrations travelled back through my body to my core. Energy flows, love grows.

Surprisingly, the neighbours didn't complain. To their way of thinking I was a handy Neighbourhood Watch device.

I kept playing and playing that drum until my hands were red raw, and the snippets of guitars and percussion instruments coming from other backyards had stopped.

My dreams that night were of jungle rhythms and primitive dancing through the decades of my life.

Now, I'm learning to actually *like* my new curves, especially my new breasts — having a C-cup is hours of fun!

And for a role model, I only need to think of Marilyn Monroe. GO, the woman who is curvaceous, sensuous, voluptuous, and other tasty words that rooooooollllll around the mouth like a ball-bearing in oil.

So girls, all together now, grab hold of your love handles and repeat after me: "I'm a little teapot, short and..."

No! No! No! Wrong affirmation! Try this one: I have the body of a goddess and I'm not afraid to use it!

Self-reliant, like the goddess Circe

November 3, 2006

I am often alone, but never lonely. There is a difference but I've got no-one to ask what it is.

Forget the love escapades on *Sex And The City* — those Manhattan girls have nothing to complain about considering they find themselves a date every second episode. The real challenge for any single thirty-something is finding a good man anywhere.

As a thirty-something singleton living in Sydney a few years ago, I realised the dearth of male attention had something to do with my insanely busy city life. I was living in an apartment the size of a dog-box, I was more likely to spend late nights at the Laundromat than a cocktail bar, and while my pet goldfish was forgiving of my long absences, he was hardly company when I did get home.

So, somewhat spontaneously I pointed my car west and drove to the other side of Australia. I wanted to find love, and if the popular Aussie television series *Sea Change* was anything to go by, I was bound to find my new hunk hanging out at a jetty near an idyllic seaboard.

I was soon to discover that the series was a fantasy. I looked everywhere from the fishing docks to the local bait store, yet my hero was nowhere to be found.

I began looking further afield, attending calf auctions where I'd heard a rumour the farmers all had 5.2 sons. Tossing my ponytail flirtatiously got me nowhere — except once when a badly timed flick won me a brown-eyed calf called Missy Moo. But other than that, the men only had eyes for their cows.

It was during yet another eye-lash batting session at the seafood co-operative that it dawned on me... if I was going to survive living in the country, I had to become the epitome of goddess Circe — the Greek goddess who lived alone on her island to pursue her love of magic.

The archetype of Circe is that of autonomous woman, self-empowered and whole unto herself. She does not need a man to complete her, although in her role as femme fatale in Homer's *Odyssey*, she did transform Odysseus' sailors to the animal closest to their true nature — pigs — to keep her company.

Now, I was quite happy to become the custodian of a calf, but not a pig (or worse, pigs.) I had already lowered my standards in so many other aspects of my life — it's the trade-off for having an internal laundry and room to own a cow.

Thus, I decided to follow Circe's example and take responsibility for my own actions, life and destiny. I was able to clench my fist and reclaim my *'Empowered Woman'*, my restored virginity and the backyard that comes with my new country life.

Each day when I take Missy Moo on her daily walk down to the jetty (sans fishermen) to watch the sun go down, I am reminded that being alone can be wonderful — thanks to Circe, I am often alone but never lonely.

U2? I'm a-Freya-d not!

November 17, 2006

What do you do when you're at a rock concert but the band thinks it's at a political rally?

I knew I was in for a doozy of an evening when our waiter wanted $10 for a garbage bag.

Spontaneous rain prior to the U2 concert in Sydney presented a calamity, you see ... one that my $400 Joh Bailey[2] haircut wasn't prepared to tackle unaided. Thus, I needed an emergency garbage bag to cover my curls.

I'm rather surprised that even with a few flirtatious flicks of my Joh-blowed tresses that the waiter didn't want to throw himself — and his garbage bags — at my mercy. Nevertheless, I rationalised his extortion with the knowledge that this was an occasion worthy of the outfit, hair and high-fashion garbage bag.

Worth it, because I suspected this would be the last time I'd be seeing the "Irish entertainers" (as they are known to the Australian prime minister, John Howard, albeit without the sneer) in Australia.

But not, as it turned out, for any other reason... I soon realised the big screen at the U2 concert wasn't meant for entertainment purposes. It was primarily used by Bono and the lads as a backdrop for political messages pertaining to World Poverty.

And, I think, harmony between the religions. I'm not entirely sure — I was tuning out by that stage...

Now, I'm all for supporting fair trade, eradicating world poverty, living with tolerance and sharing the joy, but I didn't pay $300 for the privilege of listening to singalong politics.

And definitely not at any stage was I tempted to send an SMS to the afore-mentioned John Howard on Bono's behalf. (Not even the promise of a sneak peak up Bono's shorts could tempt me — not that he was wearing shorts. And not that a sneak peak was a particularly attractive offer. And not that ... oh, never mind.)

What was a girl to do? Put yourself in my shoes — it was a Friday night, my favourite band was delusional, and the moisture inside my garbage bag was hyper-hydrating my hairdo.

It was time to call on the superpower of Friday's benefactor — the Nordic goddess of love and war, Freya.

In modern terms, Freya represents passion: Passion in love, Passion in war, Passion for the things in life that bring us pure joy. And on this auspicious occasion of the U2 political rally, this meant champagne.

Well, I learned something on Friday night. After one glass of champagne, words like 'cinnamon' and 'plethora' get a little tricky.

After one bottle of champagne, encouraging sentences like "C'arn, Bono, show us some leg" may roll off the tongue but that doesn't guarantee clarity.

But after two bottles of champagne, whole sentences become impossible to say. Sentences like, "Oh no, I really couldn't go another kebab" and "Tell that Brad Pitt look-alike he is NOT going to compromise me tonight."

I wanted to mosh, but I was fried. I was asking the guy next to me for a leg-over instead of a leg-up, and he didn't even look like Brad Pitt. Well, not at first anyway. Two glasses later he was looking the goods, though.

I won't say any more than that... my memory won't let me. But I will say that if you are feeling that you are living your life without intention, devote this Friday to its namesake. Friday is the day to get back to your passion, and get your passion back!

The mother of re-invention
November 24, 2006

Oprah Winfrey nailed it when she said, "At some point, every one of us gets out of bed, grabs a hot shower, downs a cup of coffee, goes to the closet, and decides that we haven't got a thing to wear."

Talk about extremes. On Monday I became the cover girl for Spheres magazine[3]. On the same day I donned my nail bag to help my husband build two townhouses.

In the space of two hours I was both a Joh-blowed glam queen and a nail-busted dust-bunny.

Just goes to show, a goddess gal can be anything she wants to be — whenever she wants to be it.

Oprah Winfrey nailed it when she said, "Young or old, rich or poor, country girl or city slicker — it doesn't matter. At some point, every one of us gets out of bed, grabs a hot shower, downs a cup of coffee, goes to the closet, and decides that we haven't got a thing to wear."

It's at such a time, that no matter whether you're a cover girl or a nail-bagette, a closet crisis represents the perfect opportunity to re-invent yourself. And there ain't no better archetypal goddess for re-invention, than Hathor.

Hathor was revered as the ancient Queen of Heaven. She was the patroness of dancers and the source of light and radiant power... a bit like me when I'm wielding a blow-torch on the job-site. Sure gets the lads dancing around (or ducking for cover at least.)

But seriously, Hathor brings the gift of shape shifting — she lets you transform from a woman crippled with closet-crisis to the woman you really want to be.

Next time you're standing in front of your closet, ask yourself, "who is it that I want to be today?"

That is exactly what I did yesterday morning when getting ready for another day on the construction site. I used the following colour guide to achieve the image I wanted to present:

- **Red:** As a symbol for danger, red is used for stop signs, high voltage signs, traffic lights and fire-fighting equipment. Hence, I pulled on red socks as a message to the lads on the building site: "Beware — this girl doesn't know how to operate a drop-saw."
- **Orange:** My orange knee-pads said it all — I'm enthusiastic and active about this project; my creative urges are flowing; and I'm not too serious about the situation. Which is fortunate, because I was starting to look like a rainbow. Read on...
- **Yellow:** This colour helps in decision-making; to increase confidence; and to bring some sunshine on cloudy days. For this reason, my suede brown nail bag got a lick of sunflower-yellow paint. In the shape of a sunflower. Do you think it's coincidental that my supply of tech-screws ceased being pilfered?
- **Pink:** Pink is the colour of universal love. Soft pink increases tenderness, love and acceptance; crimson raises passionate energy; and magenta helps you stand firm against disorder and pain. Or so I was hoping as I pulled on my hot-pink singlet — it's murder lugging

timber all day. It worked. The colour outed latent chivalry in the lads, and they carried the timber for me.

- **Light Blue:** My lapis lazuli pendant is designed to promote the flow of communication and to broaden my perspective of my world. This last bit happens naturally when I'm balancing at the top of the ladder, but it helps to have the added protection of light blue when it comes time to scream for help.
- **Indigo:** Dark blue helps you develop intuition; rise above the rut you have created for yourself; enjoy solitude; or find a solution to a problem. It's no wonder then, that I found that my navy-blue cell phone invaluable when lying at the bottom of a trench.
- **Purple:** Add shades of purple to your life when you want to expand your imagination, remove obstacles, and feel like royalty. Not that purple tiaras are easy to find, but don't let that stop you. It's amazing what you can achieve with a pot of paint and some Hathor-inspiration!

In a land before Eve

December 1, 2006

Lilith inspires us to stand up for what we believe in, even if we are cast as a demon for doing so.

If you ask me, Lilith had a pretty bum rap. Not only did she get kicked out of Eden for standing up to Adam, but she was replaced by the more subservient Eve who, according to popular folklore, committed the Original Sin.

Had Lilith been left in charge, well, who knows? Perhaps there would have been snake pie for dinner that evening and everyone would now be living happily ever after — without the penance of pain-in-childbirth to temper population growth.

Or perhaps apple pie would have been on the menu but anyone who had an issue with that would have been told to bugger off and we'd still be living happily ever after — imagine a world without doctors (thanks to a diet of guilt-free *pomme du jour*) and the associated medical insurance?

But as it happens, Lilith went on to bigger and better things. She became a Sumerian and Hebrew goddess honoured for her wisdom, freedom, courage, playfulness, passion, pleasure and sexuality.

Good stuff. But not in pre-2300 BC, as it turns out, where frustrated Levite priests were threatened by her assertive attitude and portrayed her as a demon.

Poor Lilith. Talk about jumping from the garden into the mulch. Fortunately for us modern chicks, Lilith henceforth became the first feminist and liberationist. She inspires us to stand up for what we believe in, even if we are cast as a demon for doing so.

Yes, we do tend to get called names when we assert our innate power — witch, control freak, Mom, to name a few — but there is a fabulous tool you can use for rising above such aspersions from others.

It's called forgiveness.

Just Google 'forgiveness' and you'll get thousands of resources telling you why this is an essential act, but basically if we *don't* forgive, it's like giving someone free rent in your head-space. They get free rein to torment you, undermine you, and kick you out of Eden.

If you're lucky in your search, you'll also come across one entrepreneurial type who is offering you forgiveness for free.

Yes, that's right. Salvation is only a click away at Get Forgiven[4], where you can "get forgiven instantly and live the life of sin without consequence" (while stocks last.)

Howard Campbell claims he learned of an 18th century shipwreck with a particularly precious cargo — 500 bales of papal indulgences — of which he was able to salvage 23 bales of blank indulgences. Like a true Christian, Howard is sharing them for free with anyone who has dabbled in any of the seven sins.

As Howard says, there is salvation for you no matter whether you've "shown excessive **pride** in your knowledge of the Kama Sutra, **envied** Howard Stern's Sirius satellite deal, ate like a **gluttonous pig** after a drinking binge, **lusted** after a neighbour, became **angry** when you caught your spouse on an Internet dating site, felt the **greedy** pleasures of trading Forex, or enjoyed a fondness for **sloth** by parking in the handicapped slot."

Pity they didn't have the Internet back in 2300 BC. This might have been a handy tool for Lilith to forgive her adversaries for their short-sightedness in giving us doctors and medical insurance.

All is love in fear and war

December 8, 2006

Living in our heart chakra, Kwan Yin facilitates forgiveness and joy. Keeping things balanced, she aids the release of guilt, trust issues and past hurts.

Google the word "love," and you get about 966 million results in 0.04 seconds.

But what is love? It's the age-old question. Even Google invite you to define it further. ... It offers sub-categories such as: love (Makes Me Do Foolish Things), love (religious views), love (cultural views), love (scientific views), Love? (Eurovision), and more...

The reason I know this is because I googled 'love' recently to get a feel for the state of affairs out there (and by 'affairs', I don't mean the extramarital kind.) Rather, I am actually in the process of writing a book about love — a manual, if you like — about the important of Self Love[5].

Now, to make sure this book is written with the aspect of balance (and I dare to borrow a quote from Isaac Newton), for every action there must be an equal and opposite reaction. And so I have discovered that where 'love' is the Universe's greatest power, the equal and opposite power is 'fear'.

(suspense music: Ba-ba-ba-baaaaaaaaaaaaaaahhhhhhm)

Bugger fear. I'm a simple, love-loving lover — why must we have an 'equally and opposite' emotion to offset love?

Why can't we all just live in harmony and joy? Is it so hard for armies to send in butter and vaccines instead of bombs and bullets? Is it better to have loved a short man than to never have loved a tall? And if love is blind, why is lingerie so popular?

To find an answer to these questions and more, I turned to Kwan Yin, mother of compassion in Chinese culture.

Her values are about cooperation, balance, harmony and trust. Living in our heart chakra, she facilitates forgiveness and joy. Keeping things balanced, she aids the release of guilt, trust issues and past hurts.

As such, she is a timely goddess for me to model my actions on right now.

Let me explain. The Internet is a wild and wonderful beast for freedom of speech, and just as it is a great avenue for messages of love, it equally and conversely functions as a soapbox for those who are living in a state of fear.

Being the sensitive soul that I am, it is sometimes easy for me to fall into fear for the pain that oozes from some blogs and articles. The empathy I feel, sadly, serves to block my creative urges, grind my teeth and sodden my wings. Not a good thing for goddess gals (nor dodo birds, but I have feeling they don't give a damn much anymore.)

Hence, the necessity of the questions that I posed to Kwan Yin — I needed to repossess my spark by finding balance, tolerance and acceptance that each one of us journeys at our own pace and willingness to love.

Like the energy of the beautiful goddess herself, her message came to me very gently.

"Anita, you have been hand-chosen to write this book," she said. "Therefore you are required to experience the truth as well as the lies. You need to face fear as well as love, which is all there really is (apart from chocolate.)"

OK, she didn't really say that bit about chocolate, but I wasn't about to let that stop me.

My question in reply?

Naturally: "Forget fear! Let me fall in chocolate!"

The Ix Chel health plan
December 15, 2006
Who needs two kidneys anyway?

You've tried crash dieting before.

What? No? Oh, come on, you were a teenager once, surely? Are you seriously telling me you have never starved yourself, buzz-cut your hair, hacked your nails to the quick and exhaled as you stepped onto the scales only to find you still weighed something?

Oh yeah, *now* you're remembering.

You can't deny that the thought of going beyond skin-deep beauty didn't appeal at some stage.

Who needs two kidneys anyway? At 16, I would imagine selling one off — not only would I have had a few extra bucks to spend on cigarettes and coffee, I wouldn't have needed that coat-hanger to pull up my zipper. And who needs 8 meters of intestines? Seriously. What was God/dess thinking when s/he gave us those miles of pipe? My theory was, go the straight route from stomach to bum hole and feel instantly lighter and skinnier. I would've happily eaten all my meals in the proximity of the bathroom if that were the price.

But enough of that. We're adults now. We only get rid of a kidney if it's for the likes of Kerry Packer.

Now that we're grown up, we need to be more sensible about things. And I mean 'proper' sensible. Not '1970s-style-mother' sensible. Remember the fads they went through to lose weight? Like standing in a belt sander machine that sent wobbly bits into overdrive and martinis into orbit. Like the pulley-systems that lifted arms and legs in robotic fashion and gave them carpet rash in unspeakable areas.

No, we're not repeating our mothers' mistakes. I'm talking about developing a rational and measured approach to healthy attitudes toward your diet, lifestyle and body-image. Just as you were 'taught' to be a certain way, you can certainly teach yourself to be another way.

You were born to be radiant. So look to the energies of goddess Ix Chel to get your budding enthusiasm positively blooming! Mayan moon goddess Ix Chel (ee-shell) is the mystery and joy of our feminine sexuality, mother of earth and all life, patroness of the healing arts, childbirth, destiny and comfortable shoes.

OK, I invented that bit about the comfortable shoes, but they do represent a willingness to be in your own skin rather than tottering around on spikes in the name of pride. Hence, my motto: If the shoe fits, at least make sure it matches your outfit.

Ix Chel carries an upside-down vessel in her hands, which represents the nourishing gift of water, our most essential life-giving element. She wears a serpent on her head, representing her transformation from the winter to spring energy — shedding her winter skin in order to blossom anew into spring to a new and fresh stage in the life cycle. Her message is that all things change — they wax and wane, ebb and flow, pile on and pile off.

So learn to go with the flow of your cycles with proud statements: "My big hips are sexy," "I adore my womanly shape," and "If the shoe doesn't fit, wear slippers."

Cheers to Rhiannon

December 22, 2006

Xmas is the magical season when the only 'magic' is the disappearing trick of all the funds from my bank account.

Is Xmas making us sick? A report from HealthDay[6] says that poinsettia plants can cause nausea and diarrhoea. Not only that, but the bright red holly berries are highly toxic, and the berries, stems and leaves of mistletoe, Jerusalem cherry and bittersweet are poisonous!

Ahhh, shoot. I guess this means I'll have to find new garnishes for my Chrissy feast this year. Like I haven't got enough to worry about already...

To me, Xmas Day means buckets of food, an IV drip feeding alcohol directly into my system, and catching up with A.D.D. nephews, deaf granddads and xenophobic Uncle Johns. It's also the magical season when the only 'magic' is the disappearing trick of all the funds from my bank account. And, it's the only time of year when you can wear red and green together and get away with it.

I do have one way of coping with it all, though. As Xmas in the Northern Hemisphere coincides with the winter solstice, it's the perfect time to remember Welsh goddess Rhiannon. She gave birth to a son, Pryderi, at Yule — the winter solstice. Another significant baby was born on December 25 some centuries later, but as much as I love my little brother, it's Rhiannon in her aspect of fertility and rebirth, transformation, wisdom, and magic that has my heart.

After all, it is Rhiannon's magical influence that helped me come up with the ultimate Xmas entertaining plan.

1. **Play some reindeer games**: The Xmas song *Rudolph the Red-Nosed Reindeer* makes a passing reference to 'reindeer games'. What are reindeer games anyway?
2. **Ask rhetorical Xmas questions**: Like, if Good King Wenceslas ordered a pizza, would it be deep-pan, crisp and even? Or, why aren't Santa's little helpers called sub-clauses? And, if Santa is really a man, why does he choose to wear crushed red velvet?
3. **Sing the blessing**: Have everyone come up with their own Xmas grace and set it to music. Make sure every genre is represented, from opera to rap. Here's mine for this year:

   Yo God, Yo de man,
   Yo alright, I'm yo fan.
   Thanks for the turkey
   And the chicken,
   And for my fingers
   That I'll be lickin.
4. **Table art**: It's not Xmas unless the dining table is laden with crafty ideas. Kill two birds with one roast potato by creating art out of the food. Turn the chunky apple sauce into a nifty replica of Michael Jackson *post* plastic surgery, or use the congealing gravy for Michael Jackson *pre* plastic surgery. Link onion rings for an edible table border, or hang the roast potatoes from the light fittings for a unique decorative hanging.
5. **Create a Xmas dance**: The older aunties love this — create a routine that lets them feel they're line-

dancing, and you'll have an instant baby-sitter for the whole afternoon.

Step One: Raise arms to shoulder height and punch the air (I call this the 'stuff the turkey' step.)

Step Two: Roll fists and spin around 450 degrees ('turn the turkey'.)

Step Three: Wave hands in the air and shake your body ('roasting turkey'.)

Step Four: Pretend you're a corncob. Pretend you're a corncob.

Step Five: Roll over and lie flat on the ground ('apple pie crust'.)

And repeat.

6. **Start some drinking games**: In the spirit of Test Cricket drinking games, apply the same rules to those at the dining table. Pour yourself a glass:

- For every person who sings along with your version of the grace.
- Every time someone grunts that "unnnnh" noise when they stand up or sit down.
- Each time someone mentions the Boxing Day test match.

Seriously, champagne is Rhiannon's proof that she loves us and wants us to be happy. So at Xmas, lift your glasses high and often... but watch out for the hanging potatoes. Cheers!

Yemaya just love this ...

January 5, 2007

Non-judgment day is near. So go ahead, follow the signs to bring in the New Year!

An A.C. Nielsen survey[7] of 22,000 people in 46 countries revealed these New Year's resolutions at the top of most people's list:

1. Get fitter (62 percent)
2. Strike a better balance between work and play (51 percent)
3. Avoid disastrous relationships (I'd reckon this would be just about everyone!)

What happened to the good old-fashioned pipe dream of losing the beach ball off your butt? Or having Brad Pitt's baby? Or getting a motorbike license? (That one has been a perennial favourite of mine for, oh, 10 years now?)

Resolutions are made with the best intentions — who doesn't make a promise to improve health, seek prosperity, fall in love and find lots of joy? And all before breakfast?

But deep down we all know a New Year's resolution is really something that goes in one year and out the other.

Have faith. Yemaya is here. West African, Brazilian and Afro-Caribbean goddess Yemaya is Mother Water, Orisha of the oceans. She protects us through all the highs and lows, even during the worst atrocities like when you make a really, really bad New Year's resolution.

She reminds women to take time out for ourselves, to nurture our own needs and to respect our deserved position in life.

That's all well and good for the New Year, but what about the rest of the year? Well, the key to making a good sticky resolution that you can actually keep resides in your goddess birth sign.

Goddess birth signs are similar to astrology in that they define who you are and what your life purpose may be. Once you understand which goddess energy is resonating strongest in you, you can then enhance these strengths to achieve the ultimate balance in spiritual and practical life. Everything you do, say or bite can be traced back to your goddess archetype.

So in between shower rituals to celebrate Yemaya's water energies, empower your inner goddess for the rest of your year with the best resolution to suit you, at www.goddess.com.au/Links/Signs_NewYears.htm (case sensitive.)

Spider Woman saves the day

January 12, 2007

Holy-saving-the-planet, Batman, is it a bird? Is it a plane? No, it's Spider Woman, weaving her mystical web across all nations and tribes.

Spider Woman? Mother of the Man of the same name? Sister? Aunt? No, and nor is she related to any of the other Spider characters in the Marvel Comics universe — Madame Web, Agony, Araña, Black Widow, She-Venom or the new Tarantula.

She is in fact, an ancient version of today's Internet. How cool is that?! Way more powerful than any dirty-squirty tarzan-rope swingy-thingy, and a million-gadzillion times more effective in bringing about world peace.

I can hear echoes of the Native American tribes now... "Holy-saving-the-planet, Batman, is it a bird? Is it a plane? Is it satellite broadband?"

No, it's Spider Woman, weaving her mystical web across all nations and tribes. In the legend of Spider Woman, she weaves two silver strands from the top of her head. One connects east to west, the other north to south, and thus, her cosmic web connects the four corners of the earth with Spider Woman as the centre.

Think of two tin cans connected by a piece of string. Now multiply it by a trillion-gadzillion and you're getting close to Spider Woman's set-up.

Forget being naughty or nice for Santa Claus — Spider Woman has it all over him for knowing what you're getting up to simply by tapping into this superhighway of filament. She only has to yell into a tin can to any one of her four children to get reports on where you are and what you're doing.

Along with her twin girls and twin boys (who later brought forth the sun, moon and stars, bless 'em), she created all vegetation, birds, animals and red, black, yellow and white people.

Ha! I'd like to see Spider Man do that! And I'd also like to see any superhero match Spider Woman for her crowd management skills.

Standing at the centre of her universal web, she's just like a big mommy standing in the middle of a bunch of bickering kids. Now that's quite an effort. I can barely manage to keep the peace between my own Boy Wonderful and his dog, yet Spider Woman is doing for the whole of humankind and beyond.

When one kid runs amok, all other parts of the web are influenced. Just this week, for example, 42.5 million 'kids' watched George W. Bush talk about U.S. troops. The consequences of this reckless behaviour include Timberlake and Diaz calling it quits, the Beckhams moving to Hollywood, and 8-year-old Bindi Irwin (daughter of the Crocodile Hunter) making her American TV debut.

Oh dear. What next? You don't need to run to the bat cave to see how Spider Woman's web links you to everything and everyone in your reality. So, behave! Listen to this creator and weaver of life, great teacher, protector, sacred guardian and Mother of all creation with a really uncanny way of knowing what you're getting up to.

Play it again, Bast

January 19, 2007

Why is it that bachelors are eligible, but spinsters are eccentric?

Why is it that bachelors are eligible, but spinsters are eccentric? This question never occurred to me until I moved to the country.

While I was living in Sydney, I was proud to be a SHIC (that's a Single, Happy, Independent Chick.) I was the quintessential 'eligible bachelor', only female. I earned a decent dollar, enjoyed a racy lifestyle and had a queue of potential partners wanting a piece of my action.

Sydney's Inner West area was chockablock with single professional women just like me — in fact, figures showed that 70 percent of female residents were single. This statistic is on par with New York's SoHo district, which is notorious for its independent and upwardly mobile single women.

So I was in for a bit of a shock when I moved to country Western Australia a few years ago. Here in this realm of white-picket fences and 2.2 children (who are all grown up and working on gas rigs 'up north'), a SHIC was definitely the minority.

It wasn't a pretty sight. Occasionally SHICs were treated with outright suspicion that their real goal in life was to steal husbands. Imagine giving up the freedom of singledom to take on another woman's used goods? Her Manolo Blahniks, maybe, but no thanks, not her man.

Invitations to dinner were a myth, challenges to a healthy round of social-tennis scarce, and forget joining the school's parents association — I didn't have the required appendage (aka a good husband) to volunteer for the working bees.

But all was not lost. I managed to find three other SHICs here who, like me, were happy being unmarried. We became good friends and created our own support network — Liz changed our light bulbs, Ann hammer-drilled our picture hooks, Calliope operated a mean remote control, and I was the best darned bottle-opener this side of a white-picket fence.

But the best thing of all, we were all happy to be inspired by the Egyptian goddess Bast.

Bast is represented as a cat-headed woman and, as the ancestral mother of all cats, is the patron of play.

I speak for the group when I say we donned purple stockings and pigtails and travelled the world at a whim. We got to watch plenty of sunsets and moonrises at the beach while the married women battled it out at the local parents association. We didn't quite get to slipping on cat masks, but overall we did enjoy getting up to as much mischief as enthusiastically cheeky kittens.

I can honestly say that doing 'playtime' with my SHIC friends, my dear goddess sisters, is the greatest way to forget the mundane side of life for a while.

Get rooted on Australia Day

January 26, 2007

Once foreigners start cramming for our entry test, they'll soon learn that no-one rides to school in the pouch of a pet kangaroo.

According to the Department of Immigration, Multiple Affairs and Long Lunches[8], nearly one in four of Australia's 20 million people was born overseas.

This is something worth thinking about today, on Australia Day. For those of us not hopping into Japanese cars to drive to Irish pubs, we're throwing British bangers on the barbie and chugging down Belgian beer while watching Chinese-manufactured fireworks on our Korean televisions. Of course, some of us are drinking Tasmanian beer, but that's because we are accepting of all cultures.

Even though Australia has a non-discriminatory immigration policy (which means that anyone from any country can apply to migrate, regardless of their ethnic origin, gender, colour, religion, height, weight or penchant for Thai food), on Dec. 11, 2006, the prime minister announced that the Australian Government intends to introduce a formal citizenship test.

Well, there goes the fun for thousands of Australian travellers who thrive on the national sport of telling lies to gullible internationals.

Once foreigners start cramming for our entry test, they'll soon learn that no one rides to school in the pouch of a pet kangaroo. They'll catch on that not everyone owns a helicopter in order to visit the neighbours. And, they'll work out that a savvy American pretends to be Canadian — we love Canadians.

There are many other lies that I suspect will be exposed in the test. To make it easier, some questions could be reduced to True or False statements, herewith:

- **True or False**: In Australia the compasses point south.
- **True or False**: If you're planning a trip to New Zealand from Sydney, you can save on airfares by waiting for low tide and wading across.
- **True or False**: Koalas make excellent babysitters.
- **True or False**: Australia invented the Split Enz, Russell Crowe and Velcro gloves.
- **True or False**: The capital of Australia is Broken Hill.
- **True or False**: The 2006 winner of the annual Hobart to Antarctica Swim was Tammie van Wiess.

If you answered False to the last question, well done. Everyone knows the winner was Dame Edna Average.

As for the other questions, if you answered True to any of them, it's time to start thinking a little more, well, how do I put this delicately? Bigger, more globally, more... Gaia-like.

The ancient Romans believed every element in the universe, whether on land, in the sea or in the sky — even it was floating in a backyard pool in Australia — was a single living entity of Gaia, the primordial Great Mother. She is our source of life, inherent wisdom and forms a common backyard to every home on the planet.

In other words, no matter where you live or travel, no matter what you eat or how you pray, no matter whom you marry or where you grew up, she is the one thing we all have in common. She is the Great Mother who connects us all, making us citizens of her one, global village.

So on Australia Day, no matter what your roots, lean over your back fence and say g'day to a neighbour for Gaia's sake.

Just remember to remove your Velcro gloves first.

The many faces of Hecate

February 2, 2007

It is never too late to start writing your own story with whatever ending you choose for yourself.

As I told my InnerGoddess* members last week, in a decision that has taken me, oh, 12 years to make, I am in the process of changing my name to better reflect who I have become. Initially I drew on the shape-shifting and reinvention gifts of the goddess Hathor to find my new name, but in a moment I'll introduce you to Hecate — another prominent archetypal goddess guiding me in this decision.

Herewith is some background info into my rationale. (Shhhhh, don't tell anyone I used rationale — it might give me a bad reputation.)

When I was a maiden I had my father's name. That name represents the happy-go-lucky, exploratory, sometimes awkward and often embarrassing years of my life.

Then came my first husband's name. I only changed my name to his in order to 'meet social expectations'. I look back now and realise the 'social expectations' were simply my fear-of-judgment misleading me into decisions I was making for the sake of others and not for me.

Nevertheless, the surname 'Ryan' represents 14 years of growing up, coming of age, a series of funky handbags and, most rewarding of all, being a mother to my gorgeous Boy Wonderful.

Now I'm on the cusp the beyond-mother stage. Yes, my son is still in high school and I'll be his mother for the rest of his life. However, he is growing out of his need to have the same surname as me. Furthermore, my second husband is also growing — out of patience, that is! He's tired of being called 'Mr. Ryan' when we go to restaurants.

So you see, 'Anita Ryan' is unsustainable on a personal level. It is a residue of a life that has served its purpose — a time of amazing and positive growth, mind you — but the time has come to adopt my 'adult' name for life.

This is where I introduce you to the crone witch goddess Hecate. The goddess with three faces, she completes the goddess triad of the Maiden (Persephone), the Mother (Demeter) and the Wise Woman (Hecate.) She walks between the seen and unseen world but resides in neither, carrying a flaming torch so she can see where other can't — into the human psyche. She is the one accompanying me now, guiding me with her torch, as I step into the goddess power I feel resonating in the name 'Anita Revel'.

Will my life change? Will people see me differently? Perhaps, perhaps not. But it does remind me of a story…

Once, a long time ago (in a galaxy far away back when I was a serial singleton), I was interested in finding out more about a single olive oil maker. I asked a friend (who knows everyone!) if she had any stats on this guy. She said, "Sure. He has a girlfriend and is the most painful vegetarian I've ever met."

Now, if Mr. Olive Oil could be summed up by a) who he belongs to and b) his worst character trait, how were people summing *me* up? What was the 'face' I was showing to the world?

My first instinct was to say 'mother' but the implication was that I was a snot-monster-incubator and that I enjoyed slavery.

Next I described myself as a 'devout career woman' but that implied I had no life outside work — people avoided me as the clock hit 5pm in case I went into meltdown.

I could have said I was a 'community member' or 'diligent volunteer', but those had overtones that I was actually twice my age.

I thought I might like to be remembered as the 'lady on the hill', but that made me sound like the mother in *Psycho*. I could have said 'ex-wife' or 'serial singleton', but both statuses describe who I did or didn't belong to.

Or maybe I was just a sum total of all my pickup lines — an angel who fell from heaven, wondering if I come here often and with a thief of a father who stole the stars from the sky.

Hecate might have her three faces representing the three stages of life, but I came to realise that human beings have hundreds of faces. And we choose the appropriate face to wear at hundreds of different times in hundreds of different circumstances through each day.

Every day brings with it a new opportunity to start again; the chance to put on a face and blast headlong into the start of the rest of our lives. It is never too late to start writing your own story with whatever ending you choose for yourself.

Living life with intention

February 9, 2007

I used to have a bad habit of waking up every morning with the thought that there must be a better way to start each day than waking up.

It was about my third twirl on the pulsating dance floor that I tripped over my stiletto heel and landed, laughing, at the feet of hundreds of party animals. All right, I'm exaggerating, there were only 10 people on the dance floor, and I wasn't laughing as much as saying "Weeeeeeeee!" on the way down — everything seems so much funnier when you add 'Weeeeeeee'.

But seeing as we were at a masquerade ball at an elite Margaret River winery, there *should* have been hundreds of bodies shaking their booty on the dance floor. Where were they? It's not like we were dancing the Mashed Potato and Moonwalk or anything, although the Chicken Dance and Nut Bush were proving to be remarkably resilient.

I should have invoked Greek goddess Artemis and her gift strength to overcome forces that inhibit or bind you. Just imagine her energy whipping a hundred people in a Funky-Dory dance frenzy, yelling at their partners, "I don't know what came over me — suddenly I'm dancing and having FUN!" And the partners yelling back, "Oh! I thought you just needed the loo!"

Thanks to Artemis, I make it my goal to live every single minute of every single day with *intention*. That way, if I don't get the courtesy forewarning that my Non-Judgment Day is near, then I can have my last few moments cherishing the fun I had, not crying over the regrets of what I did *not* do.

Waking up every morning with the thought that there must be a better way to start each day than waking up, I banish negative thoughts by planning ways to add sparkle to the lives of people I encounter.

For example, I might squirt a spray of my favourite perfume (ahem, now stored on a separate shelf from the bathroom deodoriser to avoid confusion.) Or I might put a rosebud from my neighbour's garden in my hair (liberated under the cover of darkness to escape my neighbour's wrath.) Or sometimes I write a complimentary note to my son's handsome teacher. (Note to self: Don't sign the letters "From my son" — it's a dead giveaway.)

Lately I've taken to dressing in a stylish fashion, with an iron-crease down the front of my jeans. Not so that I can look like an aspiring accountant, but so that I can present the image that I care. Matching my razor-sharp jeans with my 'good' jacket puts me in the frame of mind that I am prosperous and $45 will seem like a bargain for the selection of cheeses I purchase at the market. Putting cushions on my outdoor furniture is extravagant, but it's a pleasure to invite to friends over to salute the setting sun with a glass of Chardonnay in one hand and (thanks to the South West's volatile weather patterns), an umbrella in the other.

I use my best china (mismatched though it may be), and serve the best wine I can afford. I chew my food and take care of how my words will affect those around me. I listen to open fires. I taste the stories that travel across the Indian Ocean on the sea breezes. I see and read what people are really trying to say through body language. In short, I do anything to turn life into a pattern of experiences to be savoured rather than endured.

It's amazing the number of people I meet who act as though life is nothing but a sexually transmitted terminal disease. They are always planning for the days when they'll be old and running over people's toes with their rocking chairs instead of standing still occasionally and smelling whatever roses might be left in their neighbours' gardens.

I was the same until I stopped wearing a watch — now when people ask me for the time, I can say, "The time is Now." Sometimes it means I'm a little late for meetings, but I figure that being first to a meeting is a waste of time anyway — no one is there to appreciate my punctuality.

Silver screen icon and fearless female Ingrid Bergman described happiness as having good health and a bad memory. But I would much rather remember regrets for what I did than for what I didn't. So if falling over on that dance floor is my punishment for taking a bite out of life, well, that's the price I'm prepared to pay.

And hey, life may not be the party you hoped for, but while you're here, you may as well dance.

Gotta meet her, Demeter

February 23, 2007

Perhaps one of life's greatest challenges is to find a human customer service operator.

How many people does it take to move house? The answer is 1,001. One woman to manage the whole process, and the other 1,000 to calm her down.

Moving house is in the Top 3 sources of stress, the other two being the death of a loved one and, in my case at least, blocked shower drains.

I'm talking about this because I moved house last week and I'm *still* fending off talk of divorce and aneurysms.

I was so stressed I even spent time surfing The International Stress Management Association — a registered charity that promotes sound knowledge and best practice in the prevention and reduction of human stress. If that's the case, where are their shower-cleaning services?

There was one day when I thought there was light at the end of the tunnel (yes, I remembered where I'd packed the flashlight), but it went out. (I forgot where I'd packed the batteries.) Then, just as I thought my days couldn't get any darker, along comes the mother lode of all sources of stress: Coping Without Broadband.

Now, some of you might say the lack of money or getting sacked might be the most stressful thing that can happen to you. But consider this, my friends: NO INTERNET CONNECTION! Imagine that? NO INTERNET FOR DAYS AND DAYS AND DAYS!

It's enough to make one wonder how to cope with a real, live, verbal conversation. Or how to write a handwritten thank-you note. Or, for that matter, how to go window-shopping without a mouse, scour auctions in 3D, google-stalk without Google, or have cyber-sex without your partner seeing your wobbly bits.

As if that's not enough to cause me to blow a gasket, here's some more fodder for the stress bucket: Trying to Find a Human at an Internet Company's Help Desk. This problem is so prolific (and not just with Internet Service Providers), a Boston-based dude called Paul English set up a pretty nifty resource called the Get Human Project[9]. His mission is to find real humans at faceless companies in order to improve the quality of phone support in the USA.

Seeing his work and that of his volunteers made me think about the Greek goddess Demeter. According to Greek mythology, she got more than a little peeved when her daughter Persephone was abducted by Hades, god of the Underworld (the Underworld being an ancient version of a modern-day conglomerate.)

Demeter's search for her lost daughter took her on the path of poverty, abuse and eventually madness. She neither ate nor slept, she roamed land and sea and refused to give Persephone up for lost. But, her perseverance and determination paid off in the end — as truly devoted motherhood always does.

Armed with Demeter's determination and the support of over 1 million Get Human consumers, I picked up the phone (again and again and again and again and again) until I finally got through to the Help Desk at my Internet

Service Provider. Too bad I was answered with a recording.

"Your call is important to us," it said. (You know the drill.) "Your call will be answered within 24 hours," it goes on to say.

Pity it couldn't hear me wishing them a peak-hour transmission failure on the freeway, armpit infestations from the fleas of a thousand camels, and many other nasty things (some involving red-hot pokers.)

My Fijian-Indian friend taught me an Indian expression for times like this: "If you can't scoop the fat from the pot with a spoon, use your finger."

Well, I used my finger, all right. I used it to ring the ISP's main number again. But this time, instead of pressing '3' for tech support, I pressed '1' for sales. Funny how I was able to find a human within three phone rings this time. With customer service like this, it's time to go the way of your namesake, D----!

This gave me an idea. I used my finger again. This time I dialled another ISP, and (as expected) was signed up with a new account within minutes. Ahhhh, bliss!

Well, anyway, what I learned is that on one hand, the only real stress-free environment is in the grave. But on the other hand, if the world didn't suck, we'd all fall off. So be grateful for the occasional reminder calls that we're still alive — just make sure you answer the phone when the calls come in.

Go with Oshun's flow

March 2, 2007

Just as water ebbs and flows, so should we allow ourselves to live, being generous with our time for ourselves during an 'ebb,' and for others during a 'flow.'

You've waved your visitors goodbye, washed their sheets, hung them out to dry, remade the guest bed, added their belongings to the 'lost and found' basket, texted them to wish them a safe journey home (again), made coffee, and now you're sitting down to read a magazine.

Ahhh, there's nothing like the feeling of coming out of the other side of a major project. The change in pace, however, can be somewhat of a head-spin. I wouldn't say the head-spin is better than drugs, but it sure beats the alternative — staying stuck in the high-adrenalin ride that the project brings.

Don't get me wrong. Change is inevitable (except from a vending machine.) It's just when it's pedal to the metal one minute and floating in space the next that it can cause the grey matter to splat.

This, dear goddess sister, is the ebb and flow of how life works.

Ebb and flow? With words like that spilling out, there can be only one goddess energy resonating with me this week — Oshun. Patroness of rivers and the bloodstream, this Nigerian goddess (also brought to Brazil and Cuba) was honoured as the goddess of love and sensuality.

Love and sensuality aside (who's got time?!), it's her river energy that is affecting me this week. I've just got through a couple of weeks of visitors, the Wild Woman Weekend[10] and other workshops, moving house, birthing a book[11], getting my Boy Wonderful off to high school... now that I have Internet connection again (albeit dial-up only at this stage), it's time for me to go back into the flow of doing what I love the most: writing!

I welcome the flow!

So why am I hitting a wall? I'm normally so astute with getting my columns in on time. I take comfort that the early bird might get the worms, but I've never fancied them as part of my diet. So right now I'm more of a cheese girl — call me the second mouse who gets the cheese.

Fortunately, Oshun teaches us to 'go with the flow' in order to find inner tranquillity. She teaches us to be easy on ourselves in times of an energy 'ebb', because in true tidal nature you're just preparing for an energy 'flow'.

To Stop Drifting Along...

When you decide it is time to stop bobbing along with the bubbling brook without direction or intent, but instead to find a place where you can simply 'be,' here is one way to do it. It's a method I've shared with my InnerGoddess group before with lots of gushing feedback.

Take an orange blanket with you to a peaceful place by water. Whether it is a river, a beach, or in front of a collection of stones under your garden tap, it doesn't matter, as long as you can be with yourself in peace.

Bring an orange scarf if you don't have an orange blanket, as orange is a colour related to the sacral chakra and will bring you fluidity and grace, depth of feeling, sexual fulfilment, and the ability to accept change. (Sexual fulfilment? At this stage I must intervene to advise that no, this is not available in tablet form.)

Using an affirmation about stillness as an anchor, release your mind to wander the depths of your consciousness. Acknowledge shopping lists or 'to-do' jobs as they float into your head, but then release them so that you can focus on the 'now'.

Watch the water and let yourself wonder at its ever-changing face yet ever-constant properties.

Likewise, understand that you can also ebb and flow while keeping your essential integrity. Give yourself permission to occasionally ebb away from your chores, knowing that you will flow back to them again with renewed energy.

Follow that ass

March 9, 2007

It took a mule to show me how to listen to intuition.

I spent most of yesterday wandering around the French Quarter here in N'orleans looking for Angelina Jolie and Brad Pitt's house. Although I wasn't successful in my mission, I reckon there are worse ways to spend a day... Resisting the to-go cocktails, for example. Or digesting an overload of crawfish ettouffe. Or trying to find a better restaurant than Brennans on Rue Royale[12]... (that was a trick one – it's impossible to find a better restaurant!)

Regardless, I consider the hours I spent meandering through the historic streets well invested. I am now totally, officially, unequivocally in love with the French Quarter. The living history is phenomenal, the architecture is magical, and the people are diehard optimists. They even joke about the encroaching shoreline of the Gulf, saying that their homes will be beachfront property in 10 years' time.

Now this is the part I don't understand. If the people are expecting to have to don scuba gear to see such attractions as the Old Ursuline Convent, why are they spending millions and millions of dollars buying real estate? Angelina reportedly paid $3.5 million in cash for their home in January this year. A real-estate listing for the property shows the house has a grand spiral staircase, elevator, gourmet kitchen, private courtyard, double garage and separate two-story guesthouse. Brad Pitt came as an optional extra.

This was a mansion I simply had to see. Which is why I spent the hours honing in on my gut instinct and following where it led.

When my gut instinct kept leading me to an astonishing array of to-go cocktail bars, I changed tack and called upon the Egyptian High Priestess Isis for divine guidance.

Isis' esoteric attributes include intuition and perception. She is also related to the third-eye chakra, the centre of illumination and insight.

"Show me the way to Brangelina's house," I asked her. I was subsequently led around to view magnificent homes such as the Beauregard-Keyes House, the Cornstalk House and even the unlikely St. Louis Cathedral.

I didn't get too upset with myself that I wasn't channelling Isis well enough to find the Jolie-Pitt mansion. That's just what a modern goddess does — accepts that everything happens at the perfect time for the perfect reason. On this note, I gave up the search and instead opted for a ride in a mule-drawn carriage.

My driver was very typical of a true N'orlean. He was as diverse as the culture with his clipped N'orleans accent, Australian driza-bone coat and a mule named after an Egyptian goddess. Her name? Yep, you guessed it: Isis.

"OK," I laughed. "If you have to shape-shift yourself as an ass to get your message through, Isis, I'm listening."

With that, Isis led us directly to the house I'd been seeking all day. Although no one was home (the couple are in Vietnam adopting another baby, according to the rumours), I was at least very happy to have found success in my mission at last.

Kali vs. New Orleans

March 16, 2007

Is it fair to say that the goddess of destruction actually loves the New Orleanians?

I'm currently reading *The Five People You Meet in Hell: Surviving Katrina* by the New Orleans writer Robert Smallwood[13]. It's brutally candid so of course I'm riveted by Robert's first-hand account of the horrors of surviving in the French Quarter in the days following Hurricane Katrina.

There is one scene that struck me in particular: "The police drove off with the corpse on the hood of their car like road kill."

What struck me most about this is that this took place in the French Quarter — the historic neighbourhood that got off relatively lightly (ha!) compared to Lakeview, Gentilly and the Ninth Ward. The scene is something I'd have expected to have taken place in the outer wards of the city, not in the vivacious and historic heart of historic New Orleans.

Now, we've all gone through times when the carpet has been ripped from under our feet and we are suddenly on our tush, wondering what the heck happened to life as we know it. (We may also wonder how we came to have plush-pile carpet in our lives in the first place, but that's a whole other story.) But I am struggling to think of another time in a civilized country's history that a natural disaster destroyed the lives of 500,000 people in the course of six hours.

It would be easy to assume that a storm of this magnitude must be the work of Kali — the Hindu goddess of destruction. Typically, she is depicted wearing a necklace of skulls, blood dripping from her teeth and dancing on corpses. Not the type of girl one takes home to meet Mum, kind of thing.

But there is more to Kali than meets the eye, for it is in the act of destroying that she facilitates rebirth. That is, in destroying life as we know it, she is simply doing what it takes to get us back onto the right path — the path where we will ultimately be happier and more satisfied with our lives.

I know, I know, it can be a right pain in the neck to have your life turned upside down. I first met Kali when my first marriage started going bad. I hung in there, hung in there and hung in there some more, but it wasn't until bugalugs got *reeeaaaaal* nasty that I got out of there and started a new life.

For those of you who have also been through Kali's wringer, I'm willing to bet you can look back and recognise you are in a far better place now than then.

Personally, I now find enormous comfort in being able to ride out storms in my life knowing that they are simply Kali having a tantrum about my inertia.

But back to New Orleans and how the tragedy relates to Kali's energy.

As I told my InnerGoddess* members this week, every local that I met during my week in New Orleans said the same thing: "Tell your friends we are now dry (!!) and to PLEASE COME AND VISIT. Support our businesses, help create employment, and do what you can to help us rebuild our city."

So naturally, upon hearing this, I saw it as my duty to shop! I especially loved the knickknacks at Oonka Boonkas[14] in Chartres Street, where my big spend-up earned me a hug from the store owner and a warm, fuzzy feeling in my wallet.

Also during my week in New Orleans, we dined at the oldest restaurant in America[15], drank at the oldest bar in America[16], sat on the balcony of the oldest apartment building in America[17], ate the most famous breakfast in America[18] ... (ha ha, you thought I was going to say the *oldest breakfast*, didn't you?!)

The list goes on, but the point is, New Orleans has been around since America began to settle, and thanks to Kali's kick up the bum and the interminable, never-say-die nature of the French Quarter locals, I look forward to seeing New Orleans grow even more infamous and 'fabulouser' and in the generations to come.

Fortuna's Law of Attraction

March 23, 2007

Have you ever noticed the phenomenon that the more you give away, the more comes back to you? This is the Universe's circle of providence, constantly ebbing and flowing karmic energy.

In my column last week, I was telling you about the fascinating book *Five People You Meet in Hell*, a firsthand account of surviving Hurricane Katrina by New Orleans writer Robert Smallwood.

I'm bringing this up again because I came across one line that really opened my eyes (which sure as heck beats reading with one's eyes closed.) It was an exclamation of joy, when Robert found a stash of dry goods in the ravaged city: "Oh, Fortuna! Toilet paper!"

Now, Robert attributes this line to Ignatius J. Reilly, the 30-year-old medievalist, fat, flatulent, gluttonous, loud, lying, hypocritical, self-deceiving, self-centered blowhard hero of John Kennedy Toole's Pulitzer Prize-winning novel, *A Confederacy of Dunces*. But what has a man with a green hunting cap and a fleshy balloon of a head got in common with a Roman goddess of abundance?

Well, pretty much the same as the rest of us, in that we're often quick to blame or give gratitude about things beyond our control, to forces greater than us.

In Fortuna's case, she is invoked for good luck and prosperity, lamented to during times of hardship, or called upon when a spare wheel needs changing. Just joking about that last bit — she needs her wheel to steer our destinies.

Fortuna promises riches and abundance, but most of all she rewards those with joyful intentions with success and prosperity.

Talking about prosperity, I've met all sorts of people and seen all degrees of wealth while touring the States. I've met old money, new money and new-improved credit cards. I've met true-blue hard workers and boo-hoo-too-hard lurkers. Some people live by the seat of their pants and, providing they check out by late afternoon, have all the money they will ever need. Others are the type who risk all to win their fortune (forgetting that in order to come home with a *small* fortune, they must first leave with a *large* one.)

In most cases, the people I've met are realistic about what a dollar buys, and what they need to do in order to earn one. There are no shortcuts or 'secret' ways to get rich, but from personal experience I can tell you one way to get *poor* very quickly — just spend four nights in downtown Chicago!

Whoever said money doesn't buy happiness hasn't spent their time and cash wandering up and down the Magnificent Mile during Sale Season!

Now, before you jump in and argue that material possessions aren't the key to happiness, I happen to agree with you. I believe that while thousands of people are discovering *The Secret* and searching for answers to that elusive get-rich-quick mystery, those in the know have already worked out that abundance is not just about money and material goods.

Being truly rich is also about meeting the needs of our spiritual, physical, mental selves, and the needs of our neighbours. And in true Fortuna spirit, it's about taking care of others selflessly and with joyful intentions.

Have you ever noticed the phenomenon that the more you give away, the more comes back to you? This is the Universe's circle of providence, constantly ebbing and flowing karmic energy. So the way I see it, the more cash I can afford to spend, or the more time I can invest in helping others, the more I am investing in Universal Flow and the more that will ultimately be returned to the community at large.

This mindset isn't new. Traditionally people may have shared rice cakes with colleagues, visitors and passers-by in order to share the wealth and allow the goddess to bring prosperity into many more lives. In modern times I see the act of handing out my cash as a way to manifest benevolent goddess energy — whether it be during Sale Season or otherwise.

To turn Fortuna's wheel of fortune in your favour, choose something to share with those around you. It doesn't need to be food or belongings; it could be a helping hand or a well-timed compliment. It could be an encouraging smile, giving directions to a café with real espresso coffee or, in the hurricane-ravaged city of Robert Smallwood's New Orleans, it could simply be about buying a roll of toilet paper.

Flora's spring fling

March 30, 2007

It's time for women to celebrate their bodies in their natural states – although perhaps not in Chicago, not without reverse-cycle air-conditioning at least.

Over the last three weeks, husband 'Luvvy' and I travelled 4,500 miles, from Louisiana to New York, the long way. A wrong turn in Tennessee took us through the hills of Virginia and back across Kentucky before eventually channelling us into Chicago. That type of thing is bound to happen when you're travelling on a whim and a dare, as we were doing.

The vast comparison in U.S. weather patterns became very apparent to me during this road trip. In the South, for example, springtime blossoms were providing some aesthetic competition to thousands of Mardi Gras remnant beads in the New Orleans streets. In the North, on the other hand, Luvvy complains that he nearly lost his manhood to the biting cold in Chicago. (I still love him regardless.)

But no matter where we went, one aspect of the weather was consistent: When spring springs in America, it springs with a zing.

I could sense thousands upon thousands of people stretching and yawning and scratching their armpits. South and north alike, Americans were emerging from their doorways like lambs into the light, stepping out of their winter slumber and into the revitalising energy of spring.

Literally, at this time of year, there is a 'spring in the step' as they blink away the sleep from their eyes, fold their flanny pyjamas and welcome back the red-red-robins as they bob-bob-bobble along.

All creatures test new fur, feathers, scales, teeth, claws, skateboards and tennis rackets and head toward the invigorating energy of spring. Primal urges to reproduce kick in, as do prevailing urges to clean the nest. Abundant and fresh fruit appears in supermarkets, and the riotous colours of light and flowers make us heady with happiness.

It got me thinking about springtime goddesses who preside over fertility, new energy and growth: Maia, Diana, Artemis, Persephone and Eostre, to name a few. But in the lead-up to Beltane — a time of unashamed human sexuality and fertility — I especially reflect on the energy of the Roman goddess Flora.

Though she did not have a place in the Olympian Twelve, she was very popular with the Romans for her influence over flowers, sex and reproduction. A bit like Sophia Loren, I suppose, although she has more influence over style, sass and oversized sunglasses.

During pre-Sophia Loren times, citizens celebrated Flora's energy during a six-day festival known as Floralia. They gathered boughs and blossoms to adorn temples, statues and sweethearts' homes. Women celebrated their bodies in their natural states — perhaps not in Chicago though, not without reverse-cycle air-conditioning at least.

I'll talk more about Beltane in my columns over the next few weeks in the lead-up to the May 1 festival (in the Northern Hemisphere.) But in the meantime, one way to begin introducing Flora's happy energy into your life is to plant a bed of flowers.

If you have a garden, dig a hole in the ground of your favourite sacred space, and plant seedlings of your choice. Invoke Flora's energy and bless the new growth with the words:

> *In this season of joy and birth,*
> *and in the name of the Goddess,*
> *I gift these seedlings to Mother Earth*
> *with blissings and blessings and a big fat YES!*

Happy upside-down Easter, Eostre

April 6, 2007

What's the deal with celebrating Easter in autumn?

If it weren't for Christians and Hallmark, us Aussies would be celebrating Easter in September. We'd also be celebrating Xmas in June, Halloween in May and springtime orgies in October. (Don't believe me? You can see the Southern Hemisphere calendar at my website[20]. Don't expect any orgy pics, though — this is a family-friendly site.)

Timing is not the only upside-down thing about popular Christian holidays. My Boy Wonderful and I recently had a fabulous discussion about the 'stars' of each festival and their ambiguous sexuality.

Take Santa Claus, for example. When you think about it, he's a somewhat suspicious male, for many reasons:

1. He wears crushed red velvet;
2. His laugh is unnatural;
3. He's at home in a shopping centre;
4. He's into last-minute gifts;
5. A real man wouldn't be happy with just a glass of milk and a carrot stick — he would be raiding the fridge looking for more;
6. He has an all-female staff. (No man knows how to pack bags or boots or sleighs);
7. He drives a 12-'horsepower' vehicle at high speed, mindless of the speed limit. (The reindeer are female, too, by the way — only a woman can be relied on to

get the job done in spite of a cross-dressing, eleventh-hour and shopaholic boss.)

Boy Wonderful, to his credit, managed to counter-reason why Santa is definitely a manly male:
1. If he's lost in the clouds, he won't stop and ask for directions;
2. He makes things more commando-style than they have to be, like entering a house through the chimney instead of the door;
3. He doesn't stop people from shooting reindeer in reindeer season;

We also came to the conclusion that the Tooth Fairy is also a boy. And for more than a couple of reasons:
1. He collects ivory and stores it in his shed, waiting for the one day when he will eventually organise it;
2. He comes in the middle of the night and is gone by morning with no thanks or a contact number;
3. All he's left behind is a lousy 50 cents.

As for the Easter Bunny, well, considering he turns up any time between mid-March and April without calling first, we both agreed he's definitely a boy.

Out of all the festival mascots, the Easter Bunny is the one, enduring 'star' that stays with us day in, day out. But he does so under an alter-ego — he lives in the skies as the Lepus (hare) constellation at the feet of Orion.

Lepus' story can be traced back to Easter's namesake — the Anglo-Saxon goddess of the dawn, Eostre.

According to legend, Eostre became angry with her consort — a rabbit with an extraordinarily high libido — and cast him into the heavens. What a hot, cross bunny he must have been!

All was not lost for Lepus, however. Eostre gave him the gift of laying eggs once a year, which, combined with the symbolism of new life (Christ's resurrection), is why we have a modern-day myth of the 'Easter Bunny' delivering Easter eggs to children.

Only problem for us is, she gave him this gift in spring – new life and all that. So why do we antipodeans celebrate a spring festival in autumn? Again I say, in relation to seasonal festivals, Hallmark has a lot to answer for!

On the matter of a rabbit laying eggs, well, I'm left with one last question: When the Easter eggs hatch, what kind of animal is born?

OK, two questions. Which came first? The rabbit or the egg?

The pleasure is all Uzume's
April 13, 2007

If I were to stand in front of a crowd and dance the way Uzume did, I suspect I would be arrested. But back in the golden days of ancient Japan, this saucy goddess' bawdy dance saved humankind.

While in New York a couple of weeks ago, I had the absolute **pleasure** of meeting a sister goddess in Regena Thomashauer (aka Mama Gena), founder of the School of Womanly Arts[19] — a school that trains men and women to use the power of **pleasure** to have their way with the world. Her code word also happens to be **pleasure**. Would you have guessed?

Regena told me that she takes great **pleasure** in using the story of the Japanese goddesses Amaterasu and Uzume in her classes as an analogy of women 'before' her class (wasting away in dark caves) and 'after' (shining brightly with ravishing beauty and energy.)

To understand the analogy, it's important to review the story of the two goddesses: Once upon a time... oh, bugger it, I won't disguise the story with political correctness. I'll just tell you how it was. (Note: if blatant **pleasure** offends, feel free to search 'anygoddess.com' for 'safe' goddess info.)

Amaterasu was the Japanese Sun Goddess who, along with her two brothers, the Storm God and Moon God, governed the universe. (If she thought that was tough, she should have tried living with my three brothers!)

Anyshoe, when Storm God brother wreaked havoc in her sacred domain, she fell into depression and exiled herself to a cave.

(The lesson for modern women: Caves may be safe shelters, but they don't have electrical outlets or room service. Take great **pleasure** in your surroundings to bring some sunshine to your day.)

The other gods and goddesses realised it was kind of important that Amaterasu be enticed out of her cave, because without her sunlight the earth was covered in darkness, crops were withering and dying and food was becoming scarce.

(Lesson for modern women: It simply doesn't do to starve, no matter how 'in' the size zero trend becomes. Take great **pleasure** in food to nurture a sunny disposition.)

But no matter what they did, they couldn't bring Amaterasu out of her dark dwelling. So, in true committee style (when desperate, delegate), they called on the saucy and sassy Uzume, the goddess of mirth and merriment.

(Lesson for modern women: In the battle between good and evil, always choose to use your powers for **pleasure**. Choose laughter, love and lusciousness.)

OK, so here's where the story gets juicy. Put yourself in Uzume's position — you have a crowd of deities on one hand and a hissy-fitting goddess on the other. What would you do? I bet that flashing your fanny and knotting your breasts wouldn't occur to you as a strategy!

Well, it certainly occurred to Uzume as she danced on an upturned copper tub — she tied her kimono above her waist and began a bawdy dance. The shocked deities laughed loudly at the brazen **pleasure** she unleashed upon the crowd.

Naturally, Amaterasu became a little curious about the ruckus and came out of her cave. Well, wouldn't *you* want to see what people are screaming laughing about while you're trying to sulk?

Once outside, she spied her reflection in a mirror that Uzume had prepared earlier, and suddenly realised her beauty and the fruitlessness of hiding her glorious power.

(Mama Gena's lesson for modern women: Be more like our sister goddess Uzume: A sister goddess "is a bit naughty, often outrageous, her own unique brand of Sassy and Sexy, and she uses the power of her own **pleasure** as a way of life.")

Maia Day! Maia Day!

April 27, 2007

Next time you're swanning around a maypole, spare a thought for your Southern Hemisphere sisters.

It's so weird yet lovely to think that my Northern Hemisphere goddess sisters are welcoming the approach of summer. While I am snuggling under my blanket and patting my growing spare tire, Northern gals are emerging from their caves, sprightly, sparkly, shiny and new, Amaterasu-style.

I know, I know, this winter and summer thing is part of the Wheel of Life — it's an endless cycle of beginnings, endings and reruns *ad nauseam*. But why then, as I'm stocking up on cold-and-flu tablets and preparing for hibernation, does my mind turn to May 1 celebrations in England and the United States?

It just doesn't seem fair that millions of spruced-up guys and gals will be swanning around phallic maypoles, electing a queen of the May, creating May Day baskets, rollicking around a bonfire, or washing their face in May dew to restore beauty or, at the very least (as the single gals in the Ozark Mountains believe), help her marry the man of her choice.

But here in the Southern Hemisphere, us Aussie goddesses are preparing for Hallowe'en. Also known as Samhain, Hallowe'en is celebrated here from April 30 to May 1 and is the most sacred holiday in the Wheel of the Year[20]. This is the time to celebrate the Wise Woman and make contact with those who have passed on.

We're so serious about it, we even have a public holiday to commemorate our dearly departed around this time every year. Although the origin of ANZAC Day isn't rooted in Christianity, paganism or Hallmark (as most significant public holidays seem to be), it is "a day on which the lives of all Australians lost in war time were remembered."[21]

This energy of withdrawal and introspection is probably the reason I have been compelled to do some serious 'cave time' since returning from my tour in the USA.

You know how it is. You turn off the phones (and if you're strong, the Internet too), forget the outside world and surround yourself with the comforts of home? Delicious, inspiring and wonderfully necessary... and absolutely something my Northern sisters wouldn't associate with the onset of summer in May!

History lesson commences: The month of May was named after the Greek goddess of spring, Maia. She was the eldest daughter of Atlas and the most beautiful of her seven sisters, all of whom we can see in the night skies in the Pleiades constellation. Her day of celebration, May 1, is a day of games and feasting celebrating the end of winter, the return of the sun and fertility of the soil (and randy couples.) As summer approaches, the earth is juicy, rich, productive and magic — the perfect time to empower summer wishes with some Maia inspiration.

Errrr, back up a second! What are us Southern Hemisphere gals supposed to do with Maia's yummy summertime energy when we are heading into Winter?

To answer this, let's delve deeper into Maia's history to find another aspect (as all goddesses have.)

It turns out Maia is sometimes referred to as the grandmother of magic and as the shy and gentle patroness of mothers and nurses. I sense she also enjoyed cross-stitch and bocce, but that's a whole other story.

I reckon this aspect of Maia gives us permission to spend time in May paying special attention to our own mothers, *especially* on Mother's Day, and every other day in May, for that matter.

We can participate in a big-scale event for charity, share a fabulous breakfast, or gift a small token of appreciation. A white carnation should do the trick (as per the example of the founder of Mother's Day.)

As for me, during the entire month of May I'll also be spending some time reflecting on the wonders of *being* a mother. I'll be stepping out of my cave for long enough each evening to star-gaze and give thanks to Maia (sitting pretty in the Pleiades, the constellation located between the hunter Orion and Taurus the Bull) for her gifts of renewal, joy, mother-love and cross stitch.

Baba Yaga boo!

May 4, 2007

Halloween may have passed us by with barely a whimper, but at least I got a little something in the sack.

We just celebrated Halloween here in Australia. No, not the kind of Halloween that originated in Hallmark — that season of commercial hype, crazy costumes and the chance to dig out that makeup you wore to the gym in the '80s. We did it more subtly... by pretty well ignoring it.

By "ignoring it," I mean, there were no ghoulies wandering the streets; there were no hacked pumpkins in front yards; and there wasn't a single person looking to get a little something in the sack.

The candy sack, that is. Which is a shame, really, because I can think of 10 reasons why trick-or-treating is better than getting something in the other kind of sack.

1. Even if you're married, you'll still get some;
2. The scarier your makeup the more chance you'll score;
3. It's perfectly OK to leave as soon as you've got some;
4. Fantasising about someone else is OK because you're *all* someone else;
5. You can sit on a porch for a breather if you get tired;
6. You never have to do the same person twice;
7. It's kind of fun if the kids join in the moaning and groaning;
8. Even if the goodies get stale you can still enjoy them;
9. Remaining anonymous is normal;
10. You can do everyone in the neighbourhood!

Now, of course, heathens may have ignored Halloween in the Southern Hemisphere, but not the Pagans. No matter what they call the festival — Samhain, Shadowfest, Martinmas, Old Hallowmas (even Halloween!) — they celebrated the threshold of winter and the implied open invitation for the dead to mingle with the living.

Not that the return of souls is anything to be frightened of. In fact, there are plenty of resources out there showing that you've got more reason to be afraid of some live people. The good (dead) people of Brisbane, for example, celebrated with a zombie walk a little early on April 1, but I think they were just joking. The April Fool's thing is a whole other story, though, but I ain't about to argue about it with a (live) dead person.

No, no, no... you can't be afraid of dead people. On the contrary, the lesson of the old Slavic crone goddess, Baba Yaga, is that it is only through examination of our dark side that we can hope to be reborn. It is in crossing the comfort zones and visiting our shadowed selves that we can empower ourselves spiritually, psychologically, emotionally and physically to be reborn again.

Her energy is particularly prevalent at this time of year, as she is the goddess of death and birth who sings while sprinkling corpses with the Water of Life to let them be reborn. I'm not sure what it is that she sings, but I'm fairly certain it wasn't *Somewhere Over the Rainbow*.

Or maybe it was! Who can say? In any case, she may have sung over corpses, but I say each to their own. In fact, I feel that it is quite a positive energy — rather than looking back with regret, one can look forward to new opportunities ahead.

I think this energy is carried over from ancient times... Imagine: You've just finished bringing in the crops; you're pooped; the good wife has stocked up on soup, and your mate has stocked up on beer; and it's Samhain. Now that the harvest is in, it is the perfect time to give gratitude to the goddesses of harvest, ponder achievements and look forward into the coming year. Hence, Samhain is also a time to speculate about the future.

Popular tools for divining the future included mirrors, crystal balls, flame and Persephone's pomegranate/apple, whose seeds form a natural pentagram. Many single women enjoyed using an apple to divine who their future husband would be. Herewith, the method:

Spell to divine future love

Depending on your apple-peeling skills, you may need up to a basket of apples (be prepared to bake apple pie!) Begin by blessing your apples with a chant to Persephone.

Maiden of virtue and dark skies
Let the shapes materialise
Show me clearly what's to come
As I will, so be it done.

Peel an apple in one continuous piece. If the peel breaks, finish your task and try another one. Once you have a complete, unbroken peel, throw it over your left shoulder onto the kitchen floor. The peel will form the initial of the name of your future life partner. If you know who it might be, don't be shy — invite that person over to share your Samhain feast (and lots of apple pie.)

Blodeuwedd the Beuwdiful

May 11, 2007

The Welsh goddess Blodeuwedd may have been watching too many soaps, in which case there's no surprise she slept with the pool boy.

This week, the InnerGoddess♦ gals have been talking about Blodeuwedd, a Welsh goddess whose beauty is said to be skin deep. (Who needs a beautiful pancreas anyway, right?)

The story goes that two magicians created Blodeuwedd (bluh-DYE-weth) out of flowers to be a wife for Welsh hero Llew Llaw. Her beauty proved to be only skin deep, however, when she betrayed him for the sake of a lover. Must have been watching too much *Melrose Place*, in which case there's no surprise she slept with the ancient equivalent of the pool boy.

The magicians discovered her treachery and, showing mercy, transformed her into an owl. Blodeuwedd's journey from youthful radiance to her nocturnal existence therefore represents the evolution of beauty — blossoming youth eventually wilts, but with this comes the wisdom of age.

With the cover of every gossip mag plastered with the equally trashy (and plastered) celebrities lately I can't help but wonder about the media's obsession with youthful beauty.

Sure, Paris Hilton may be pretty, but if she had any sense, would she still be an 'it' girl? If Nicole Richie swapped her weight issues to focus on weighty issues, would she still be in the public eye (apart from when she's turned sideways, that is?) If Lindsay Lohan counted, would she be shocked at the number of times she's been in and out of rehab?

It's a sad message that we're sending our goddesses-in-training: "Being popular means being pretty, naughty and empty of obvious brains."

Out of interest, I asked my InnerGoddess members: "What do you love about yourself? Is it physical, emotional, spiritual, brain-ial or an uncanny knack to smell a closing-down-sale from 100 yards?"

Oh, what a refreshing question! For so long we've been taught that it's a 'sin' to brag, or a 'deadly sin' to be vain. But it is only now, since I have asked for my members to be loud and proud about their assets that I've been able to see the groundswell of women embracing their older, wiser and wider selves. There is a certain, yummy power in acknowledging that youthful beauty is fading and it *doesn't matter*!

Here are some of their answers that have been posted at my blog♥:

- I love my kindness, my eyes, my spirituality and my butt! :-) I also love my smile.
- I love being a good mom, and I LOVE the way I look.
- I love my belly. For it is where I carried my children. And the memory is but a touch away. I have been through the hell of menopause. And it is so beautiful on the other side. I love my heart. My arms open wide and welcome all in. (I am over 50.)

- I love that I'm now getting to the stage where I'm comfortable with where I am in the journey. (And, I'm finally (!) cool with my curves.)

There is a saying that goes: "You don't love a woman because she is beautiful, but she is beautiful because you love her."

I disagree. This is not the only time she is beautiful. It is my firm belief that any woman who is connected with her authentic Self (her 'inner goddess') is beautiful, ALL THE TIME, even when she's just got out of bed and her hair is wild, or she's just picked the kids up from school and her track suit could do with a wash, or she's been sitting by a hospital bed for 48 hours straight to keep a loved one strong.

I'm not alone here – my beautiful goddess sister, Lucy Cavendish[22], has trained her friends to say "you look beautiful when you cry." It works, too!

Forget the 'Fountain of Youth'... let love, fortitude and integrity be our code for eternal and radiant beauty. We were born with these attributes, so let's dry our wrinkly eyes and allow our gorgeous-ness to shine.

I look forward to the day when men, women, the media and even the man in the moon can see the true beauty lying within all women, because this is the day when we can claim we have true respect.

What will precocious starlets do for attention then?

Dial a date with Cordelia

May 18, 2007

You know how it is... Daddy wants you to marry for affluence, whatever happened to old-fashioned love?

You know how it is... Daddy wants you to marry for affluence, but as the Queen of the Fairies you want to marry for love. And why shouldn't you? After all, this is what the Welsh goddess of flowers did!

Also known as the Queen of May for the flowers that bloom in her honour, Cordelia defied her sea-god father's wishes and married the man of her choice. In doing so, she sent a very clear message that despite her florid and joyful energies, every girly goddess has the power to stand firm on issues that matter.

Of course, Cordelia had one advantage over all the single goddess gals out there. She had a couple of men to choose from!

Personally, in a world where single chicks shop online for their groceries, music and meditation software, I can't help but wonder if Cordelia were a single goddess without a hope on the horizon, would Daddy have been happy had she found love on the Internet?

I mean, why not just skip the whole Daddy-wants-me-to-marry-Exhibit-A-but-I-want-to-marry-someone-else debacle by starting a relationship where *everyone* starts on a level playing field — in an Internet chat room?

Imagine your shopping list: "I'll have a brainiac Adonis with exceptional sporting abilities, please. Oh, and already rich. Actually, may as well make him older too — as I'm approaching my late 30s, I need to fast-track a Plan B to look after me in my early retirement."

My friend Sally (name changed to protect the shamefaced) could write a book on the Internet dating scene. She was so desperate to get the whole relationship experience, from gushy first lust to painful last gasp, that she submitted herself to a six-month period of intensive cyber-dating.

With the keen gusto of an over-enthusiastic novice, she wrote a polished and professional profile for the classifieds. It looked unwittingly like a job application:

Ten years experience in managing domestic logistics, able to forward-plan events with inbuilt contingency plans, excels in team building in accordance with Occupational Safety and Health principles and Equal Opportunity legislation.

But then again, it was eerily apt — the whole process was like a series of high-stress interviews anyway.

For Sally, the anticipation of getting home and booting up her love connection was irresistible. Gym sessions, brunches and Sunday shopping were all forgotten in the pursuit to hear the moans of her love-line warming up — the bbrrr-iii-ooo-eee-grrrrrrrr of her Internet connection was music to the ears as she kicked off her shoes and settled in for an evening of chock-a-block emotional rush.

The adrenaline brought on by an androgynous "You've Got Mail" alert was addictive. It drove her to circle more and more possibilities in the Wanted ads. Anything that looked halfway decent was sent a resume with a template letter of application:

Dear Sir(s), I read your profile with interest, and believe I have the skill-set required to meet your key selection criteria.

Computer dating meant now she could eat Spaghetti Napolitana with one hand while tapping out urgent love notes with the other. As fast as she could send them out, in came the replies.

Most of them were sweet, heart-stirring, flattering and flirtatious, validating her worthiness as a human being. Some were just photos of penises in various states of arousal. Most were horifik ecksamples of wi sum men dint have a gurlfreind.

But they all got a go, in accordance with Equal Opportunity legislation. Every single cyber dude was interviewed by email, then by phone, and if agreeable to both parties, a third-stage interview was conducted at a mutual meeting point.

Each time the cyber-dude turned out to be a reality-dud, my friend would become more and more dejected.

"Sow seeds," I'd suggest. "If Cordelia can marry the man of her choice, plant a flower-garden to invite her energy in."

Six months and a thousand failed applications later, my friend started to come around to my way of thinking.

"Plant a garden," she mused over a Sunday brunch. "What kind of credentials do I need for that?"

Survive life's cycles with Ceres

June 1, 2007

As the wheel of the year turns, pray your cycle doesn't get a flat.

Brooke Shields told George Stephanopoulos on ABC's *This Week* that there is an "entire population" of women who suffer from the baby blues — far more prevalent than anyone wants to admit.

In fact, there is an 'entire population' of women who suffer from *all sorts* of blues — try, "my favourite pants won't fit anymore" blues, the "husband didn't come home again last night" blues, the "in-laws are arriving in five minutes and I still haven't made the beds" blues, and "the celebrities think *they* have it tough?" blues.

Energies ebb and flow; that's just a fact of life. One day you can be as high as a teenage celebrity, the next day as down as a duckling ripe for the plucking. If you're having trouble coping with the highs and lows, though, Roman goddess Ceres represents the cycles we experience as women and allows us to accept the ebbs and flows graciously.

(Yes, even during PMS, when stabbing your boyfriend in the left ear with a pair of blunt scissors seems like a perfectly polite way of saying "No thanks, I do not want cream in my coffee.")

Earth Mother Ceres is the Roman name of Demeter, the Greek goddess of agriculture. The ancient myth about Ceres (aka Demeter) and her stolen daughter Persephone helps explain the cycles of seasonal change.

During the time Ceres/Demeter was searching the world for her beloved Persephone, she was so grief-stricken that she struck the Earth barren — these were the winter months. Once she had found her daughter and had negotiated her return from the underworld for six months of each year, she was happy and allowed the earth to be fruitful — and so we have spring and summer.

You see the emergence of cycles? Summer fades to fall, which falls into winter. Spring springs forth and blossoms into summer. Summer fades to fall, which... you get the picture, right? High tide/low tide; daytime/night-time; long skirts/short skirts; fat pants/fatter pants — there's no avoiding the naturally occurring cycles of life.

If you're having a low day and it's peeving you, think of the Maori proverb that goes along the lines of, "Turn your face to the sun and the shadows fall behind you."

Now, any Aussie mum will tell you that if you turn your face to the sun you will get freckles (or skin cancer, depending on how macabre your mum is.) But assuming the proverb meant well, and assuming I'm reading it right, no matter how gloomy things might appear to you, look to the bright side to leave the blues behind.

If you have the "I've got a raging chocolate craving" blues, for example, or the "I've told my child not to interrupt unless he's broken a leg or set the kitchen on fire but he interrupts anyway" blues, cheer up. Ceres encourages you to honour that need and do what you really want to do today. Go finish that oil painting, doodle in your journal, shop for brand names, or get a glamorous makeover. (Go wild. If it's bad, don't worry! Hair *always* grows back — it's part of the cycle!)

Speaking of drunken bilge rats...

September 14, 2007

On International Talk Like a Pirate Day, remember: Pirate lingo is rich and complicated, sort of like Paris Hilton but complicated instead of simple. Savvy?

I'd just finished watching the third instalment of *Pirates of the Caribbean* with my son when it became apparent we'd slipped into pirate lingo. Boy Wonderful's simple request for food, for example, became:

Boy Wonderful: "I need some grub in me bung-hole, yer dirty, land-lubbin' son of a Captain's bilge rat."

Me: "Bwaarck! Polly wanna cracker?" (Oh, wait. That's for Talk Like a *Parrot* Day.) No, what I really said was: "If it's a bucket of slop yer after, there be some swill through yonder galley porthole," except said in the accent of Tia Dalma (the character in the aforementioned movie who is actually the goddess Calypso bound into human form), so it came out more like, "a-haa-me-darrr-la-deerr-me-hiiiy."

Arrrr, it was funny, so it was! In fact, so funny we jumped onto the rigging (the pirate word for 'net) and looked up some pirate themes to create ourselves a harr-harrrrr-me-beauty 'Pirate Day' to enjoy whether land-locked or on yonder blue seas.

First things first, we needed a pirate name. There were several ports of call offering pirate names, but the first one gave me Captain Anne Kidd[23]. Shiver me timbers, how boring. The second one was a little better with Pirate Ursula the Bitter[24], but by far my favourite name (which I've since kept) is: **Dirty Left Eye Lisa**.[25]

Arrrrr! Boy Wonderful (aka **Iron Jimmy Jailbird**) and I sailed on through perilous sites of known procrastination and past rocks upon which sirens sang songs about time-wasting in search of more pieces of eight.

Risking scurvy and toe jam, we clicked on maps that were more often than not bogus, we broadsided dial-up directions, and thanks to the winds of good fortune, discovered that there was actually an International Talk Like a Pirate Day already in existence. There was more diggin' to do, though, as this information came to us via the unlikely 'What's On at The Butterfly Club'[26] events page, which was fabulous for cabaret fans in Melbourne, but not so good for those with a desire to haul some keel elsewhere around the world.

Then, with shovels-a-shovelin' and sweat-a-pourin' offava our necks like we was nothin' more than the underbelly of a taste of the Cap'n's daughter, we stumbled across the treasure: the home page of the official ITLAP Day[27].

Founded in 1995 by "two crazy guys" (or, in pirate language, "a pair of rust-buckety hornpipes with barnacles for brains," or, in parrot language, "Mark Summers and John Baur"), International Talk Like a Pirate Day was established on Sept. 19 for no other reason than "it was Mark's ex-wife's birthday, and the only date he could readily recall that wasn't taken up with something like Christmas or the Super Bowl or something."

Naturally, we weighed anchor here for a bit and picked up a great swag of pirate words (the five staple words being Ahoy! Avast! Aye! Aye aye! and Arrrr!), pirate tips and even some pirate pick-up lines (which I've banned

Iron Jimmy Jailbird from using… not because he's too young, but because they're so bad.)

But nowhere could I find any real clues about the plot of *Pirates of the Caribbean, At World's End*. Days later and I'm still asking: What the heck business did Tia Dalma / Calypso have by turning into a 60-foot seething mass of rabid crabs? The real goddess Calypso, as Odysseus will attest, simply would have kidnapped Barbossa for seven years of sexual imprisonment. Then Zeus (let's equate him to Davy Jones in the movie) would have sent the messenger-god Hermes (let's say, Captain Jack Sparrow) and… oh, never mind, this is now getting as senseless as the movie's plot.

I'm all for keeping it simple. At least I can be happy that a goddess was featured in a mainstream blockbuster (yaaarrrr!), and that she sent those swaggerin', salty, scurvy dogs a walkin' the plank for a nice, long sleep with the fishes. YAAARRR!

How to have a productive affair

October 19, 2007

I'm married to Mike Areer (but having an affair with Leisure). What has Dana, the Irish fairy queen, got to say about that?

Being married to my career (affectionately known as Mike Areer), I never expected to find a civilisation where the word *deadline* does not exist. Nor did I expect to find the attitude where *I'll do it tomorrow* really means "I'll do it when I get around to it and only if there isn't an off-shore wind." But I did find it, right here in the south-west of Western Australia.

As to whether this is a good thing depends on where one's priorities lie. A Sydney culture of murders and executions – ah, I mean, mergers and acquisitions – does not sit naturally in the more relaxed rural setting. On the other hand, a workday that starts at nine and finishes at five would not promote prosperity in the material city.

So which to choose? Career or Lifestyle?

When I was first offered a Marketing Guru role in Australia's own corner of heaven, Mike and I moved here thinking I could have both. A challenging and satisfying career marketing wine by day, and rollerblading, dog-walking and beach frolics by evening.

Together Mike and I threw ourselves at this opportunity. We learned to like the instant coffee prolific in country offices, we adapted to alcohol-free lunches, and we ploughed money back into the local economy by renovating our home (even if we had to trawl the tradesmen off the beaches to do so.)

Over the six months of renovations, the habit of going to the beach slowly became an addiction, and I found myself heading to beach even on days when I didn't need a tradesman.

It took me a good year to realise that Mike Areer and I were slowly drifting apart. Our demise started out as little niggles: "you don't stay late anymore," or "you never eat take-away with me anymore."

Mike Areer's complaints started getting louder once he realised I was becoming more and more attracted to someone else: Leisure. "You spend more time with Leisure than you do with me," was his daily nag.

Then, in the heat of a January day, a book of *Business Administration For Dummies* flung carelessly onto the sand next to me, Mike Areer issued me an ultimatum: "It's him or me!"

And there it was. The decision I didn't want to make – the security of a weekly pay cheque versus the adrenalin of catching a wave. But Mike Areer was right, of course. I couldn't continue expecting our relationship to get stronger if I couldn't focus on building it.

So, drawing on my rash-decision making skills, I told Mike Areer that while I was young and still relatively fit with only one tyre around my middle, I would be exploring life with Leisure for a while.

"Go jump in the lake," he sulked. So I did, strapping on water skis and whooping the cry of a girl who's just discovered freedom.

"Too much of a good thing can be wonderful," Mae West once said, and I am grateful I had the opportunity to live by her maxim.

But six months into my affair with Leisure and, like all relationships based on lust, my passion started to wane. As did my bank balance. I discovered this when I went to buy Mike Areer suck-up flowers and my credit card bounced.

So, it was time to go back to the marital home and see if I couldn't make amends with Mike.

Only problem was, I didn't want to go back to 'the way it was' – early starts, late finishes and nothing but a hard slog in the middle. I wanted my work to be fun, meaningful and prosperous. In other words, a career infested with sparkle, zing and magic.

To help me find all of this, I turned to the ancient Celtic version of a life coach – the goddess whose name means 'wisdom' or 'teacher': Dana.

Dana is the mother goddess of the Irish fairy people, the Tuatha Dé Danann (too-ha-day-dah-nan.) They were skilled in art, poetry and magic, and ruled Ireland until they were overrun and driven to live in fairy mounds. She is celebrated at Beltane (October 31 in the southern hemisphere), the season of fertility and prosperity when the Tuatha Dé Danann had first set foot in Ireland.

Sadly there are no recorded stories of Dana -- evidently her latent message is to tell your story before it is too late! And so, it was her magical fairy energy that spoke to me when I picked up a pen and began writing about my experiences.

'They' (whoever 'they' may be) say that a writing apprenticeship is one-million words. I sense that I have written that *and more*, but I have well and truly lost count.

What I can tell you, however, is that in penetrating the veil of 'what a career *should* look like', and instead honouring my creative destiny, I have found myself in the Land of My Heart's Desire.

In answering my calling as a writer (of many genres), I now know the key to a successful career is to have a healthy dose of fun while doing whatever it takes to achieve success.

Letting yourself have fun naturally inspires you to be more creative, more innovative, and more receptive to new and imaginative ideas. And those elements can only add a positive and permanent quality to any relationship.

Blessed be to that idea!

More information

For more information about ancient goddesses and their influence on us modern goddesses, visit: www.goddess.com.au

Get your weekly fix of goddess inspiration by becoming a member of the 'innergoddess' group. This is a free service to ensure the resource is widely available to world-wild women. Subscribe at: goddess.com.au

Thank you for supporting the website and ensuring it remains a free resource.

About the author

Anita Revel has been writing her 'Outing the Goddess Within' columns for United Press International since 2006.

She is the creatrix of the internationally popular Goddess Playshop™ and the website, Goddess.com.au – both aimed at helping you connect with your beautiful, sassy, intuitive, lovable, sacred and authentic self.

Anita has incorporated her journey into hundreds of articles, countless websites and numerous books.

In 2006, she appeared on the cover of Spheres magazine with her 'Seven-Day Chakra Makeover', and thanks to a very fertile 2007, many more books and feature articles are on the way.

Anita lives with gratitude in sunny Western Australia with her three heroes: her Super Man, her Boy Wonderful and her dyslexic god.

Other books and products by the author
Available from Goddess.com.au

Already birthed...

- *The Goddess Guide to Chakra Vitality* (Anita Ryan-Revel) ISBN 0-9757451-9-0 (US English ISBN 1-4116-5515-X)

- *Selena's Crystal Balls, A Magical Journey Through the Chakras* (Anita Ryan-Revel) ISBN 9-780975 7451-6-8

- *Chakra Oracle, Goddess Guidance For Life* (Anita Ryan)

On their way to the Delivery Room, by Anita Revel...

- *The 7-Day Chakra Workout*
- *Sacred Vigilance, Wide-Awake Meditation*
- *The Goddess Diet: See a Goddess in the Mirror in 21 Days*

View the "iGoddess" meditation movie

As Anita was doing her morning rites one Monday morning, she spontaneously began with "I, goddess..." She didn't know what she was going to say next, or why she even started with those words.

"Nevertheless," says Anita, "I trusted that if I stepped into the flow, goddess would speak."

And so She did... The meditation video that features at igoddess.com is the subsequent poem that was gifted to Anita. The movie achieved many honours at YouTube, including #1 Most Linked (31 Oct 07) in the 'People & Blogs' category. Please, enjoy…

Additional and cited resources

- ♥ Anita's Blog: goddessgoodies.blogspot.com
- 1 Read the 'How to Marry Yourself' article at SelfLoveAffair.com
- 2 Hairdresser to the stars: www.johbailey.com.au
- 3 The last few remaining copies of Spheres magazine (issue 16) are available at goddess.com.au/store
- 4 getforgiven.com
- 5 Stay informed about the release dates for *The Goddess Diet, See a Goddess in the Mirror in 21 Days*, at TheGoddessDiet.com
- 6 healthday.com
- 7 www2.acnielsen.com/news/20061228.shtml
- 8 immi.gov.au/media/fact-sheets/02key.htm
- ♦ groups.yahoo.com/group/innergoddess/
- 9 gethuman.com/us/
- 10 An annual event held in Western Australia – keep an eye on Goddess.com.au for details
- 11 *Selena's Crystal Balls, A Magical Journey Through the Chakras* available at Amazon.com
- 12 brennansneworleans.com
- 13 myspace.com/robertsmallwood
- 14 helpthecityofneworleans.com/shops-I-P.htm
- 15 antoines.com/history.html

16. atneworleans.com/body/blacksmith.htm
17. jackson-square.com
18. brennansneworleans.com/typicalmenu.html
19. mamagenas.com
20. goddess.com.au/Calendar.htm (case sensitive)
21. culture.gov.au/articles/anzac/
22. lucycavendish.com
23. piratequiz.com
24. gangstaname.com/pirate_name.php
25. blogthings.com/piratenamegenerator
26. thebutterflyclub.com
27. talklikeapirate.com/about.html

www.ingramcontent.com/pod-product-compliance
Lightning Source LLC
LaVergne TN
LVHW011422080426
835512LV00005B/202